"You"

A Theory of Self

Written by

James H. Washer

Athens, Ontario, Canada

To Stuart Bechman

FROM James H Washer.

Original manuscript composed 1988
by James H. Washer

Digitized & Edited
by James S. Washer

Questions & Comments:
jwasher@sympatico.ca
www.youatheoryofself.com
IBSN **978-0-557-00667-0**
Cover Art: James S. Washer
Illustrations: James H. Washer

Printed in the U.S.A.

YOU

A Theory of Self

Table of Contents

Chapter 1
The Source

Each of us is at the centre of a sensory web that reaches out in all directions. Eyes, ears and nose collect information from beyond our skin. Heat and pressure sensors in our skin provide information of more tactile contact with our environment. Our conscious existence is at the foci of an invisible sensory network that extends as far as the eye can see, the ear can hear and the nose can smell.

This is the natural sensory envelope with which we are each endowed. It is limited not only in distance from the centre but also in the activity level of the sensors. That is, the sensitivity of any sensor varies with the individual; some can see better than others and in some a sensor may not operate at all. Also, each sensor is limited to an intensity or amplitude level of stimuli, below which it will not respond. The eye can only respond to a small fraction of the total electromagnetic spectrum, and only from the direction it is looking; the ear can respond to only a small fraction of the total sound vibrations available; the nose is rather insensitive and limited to down-wind or relatively still air. The sense of taste principally mediates what we voluntarily ingest. All of these receptors of external stimuli are located at or near our body surface, where we interact with our external environment.

Nerves connect the surface receptors to the brain. The brain is carefully shielded, by bone and fluid, to protect it from the outside world. No external stimulus is intended to reach the brain directly. External affects that stimulate a surface sensor are carried to the brain by chemical processes along nerve pathways. To a sensitive electronic probe they appear as single "blips" that vary in frequency to the amplitude of the stimuli. For example, a light-sensitive cell of the retina will begin to blip when its threshold level has been reached. As the light intensity is increased the blip rate increases. The amplitude of the blips does not change. All nerve pathways appear to carry the same types of signals and it is the location in the brain of the cell being stimulated that differentiates between sight, sound, smell, etc... The brain gives "meaning" to what the sensors detect.

This natural sensory web of ours has been extended by artificial means; telescopes, microscopes, mass-spectrometer, light and radio interferometers, etc, now dangle from the sensors of the human brain enlarging our view by factors of millions. The sensory range of the perceived universe is limited only by our ability to devise the machines which probe its make-up.

In addition to the five external sensors we also have internal sensors. In the inner ear, orientation and motion detectors let us know when we're upside down - slightly off vertical or when the body is being subjected to an acceleration force or angular moment. We have a sense of the positions of our arms and legs - you don't have to look at your arm to tell if it is hanging at your side or sticking straight out from the shoulder. This is a gravity assisted sense, in space you have to look to be sure.

Most of our internal sensors operate below conscious level and "automatically" monitor and regulate internal organ interaction. Carbon dioxide level is being maintained at about 5.6% of air volume inside the lungs. Blood pressure, flow rate and volume to various organs, temperature, ph level, sucrose level and a host of other factors are being monitored and regulated by the "unconscious" brain, - all automatic! You'll be looking for something to eat or drink within the next four hours because you're going to "feel" thirsty and hungry. You'll need to be looking for a bathroom before too long.

All of these activities of the body are being mediated by chemical signals. Directly, for general control by hormones, or for specific control, by nerve impulses, (ionic chemical changes that sweep up or down the nerve axons). The physical acts of all organs, from the smallest sphincter, heart, lungs, glands or the act of moving the entire body, are all caused to occur by various chemical messages (symbols) interacting with chemical sensors of the many organic tissues. No conscious thought is required to go on living. Provided with a feeding tube and a moderate amount of reasonable care, the comatose body may live out its allotted 3 score and 10 and be none the wiser for it, quite unaware of its being, a tragedy for its caretakers.

The sensory web may be visualized as being a sphere within a sphere, with the brain and mind located at the centre. From the brain outward, the shell of the internal sphere is defined by our skin and represents the internal environment - our body. The outer sphere is the external environment and begins at the skin's outer surface and extends as far as the external sensors can detect. This sensory field may also be pictured as layered in concentric shells.

The visual sphere is the largest, typically the horizon (3 miles); audible sphere about half a mile; Olfactory (nose) about 5 ft.; Heat about 1 ft.; Pressure and taste, body contact. These dimensions refer to the practical daily use of a sensor. The eye has no difficulty seeing stellar objects that are billions of miles away. The skin has no trouble detecting the Sun's heat from 93 million miles. The nose can smell a coal-gas plant from 10 miles down-wind.

At the body surface, the incoming external stimuli are converted to nerve impulses by the sensors. Below the body surface, a web of sensory nerves threads through the internal environment and homes on cell nuclei in the brain.

Because we are born into a universe which has been here countless billions of years, we often get the impression that we are separate from it. But our bodies, brain included, are as much a part of the universe as the stars and atoms themselves. Our bodies are made from the stuff of supernovas; the elements make up every cell of every organ of our body. Billions of years have passed in the slow coalescence of matter into the planet Earth and the slow evolution of some of that matter into a living being.

We are very much a part of the universe and not separate from it. Our bodies conform to its immutable laws. To understand the universe you must understand that your body is an integral part of it; that the body is a multi-organed life form that has become aware of the world and its "self", through the processes of that mystical organ, the brain: that initially, the brain gets all its information from sensors via a network of nerves carrying a single type of chemical signal; and that the brain is uniquely separated from the external and internal physical world by its means of receiving and transmitting information via nerve impulses.

The brain services and is serviced by the bodies internal environment. The only way external stimuli are supposed to reach the brain is through the chemical barrier of its nerve pathways. There is also a blood-brain barrier in the circulation system designed to exclude toxic chemicals from the brain's food supply which is mainly sugar.

To be "aware" one must have both consciousness and memory. It is possible to be conscious without the faculty of memory but there would be no sense of self. Memory is a chemical-physical function of the brain. The brain somehow stores symbols, that we call memories, in its physical structure. We do not yet know how this is done or how it retrieves this information. But it has been demonstrated, during brain surgery that with pressure or mild electrical stimuli, memories of past events may be triggered repeatedly by probing some given spot on the brain. Tastes, odors, sounds and even whole scenes can be vividly recalled, repeatedly, similar to placing the needle of a phonograph repeatedly on the same location of a record.

Your body (brain included) is a self regulated chemical machine of marvelous complexity that, given the opportunity, will feed and reproduce itself. It had its genesis in the union of your father's sperm and your mother's egg and grew into its present condition from a genetic code manipulating the food, air and water it ingested. But it is the conscious "you" that is of most interest.

Who and what are "you"? How did "you" get trapped inside that mortal body? When it dies, and die it must, what happens to the wonderful you? Where did "you" come from and where will "you" go? You sort of know what I'm saying. You can read and understand the words, but now their meaning may be obscure. That is because I'm changing the focus from the physical you to the spiritual you and "self" has always been difficult to define.

Your personality, your id, your soul, the inner you, the ego, the essence of your being! The "you" who does not have a physical existence outside your body, but is so powerfully felt as real presence, that we've given it all these names. Each of us is aware of this inner self, and for many of us that inner self is the real "me". Most of us accept the short-comings of our bodies as the vagaries of fate; that it was mere chance that put "us" in the body of a pauper rather than a prince, as we deserved.

The spirit, the real "me", could inhabit any body; it all depended on luck or maybe reincarnation! Not so.

The concept of self, "you" if you like, began shortly after the most important invention of human kind; language. That's right, language! Fire and the wheel are trivial in comparison. Besides, fire wasn't invented, it was discovered. Fire was here before us. We invented the ways and means to produce fire and learned how to control it. We invented the wheel and language and mathematics.

Numbers are used to represent things in their quantities or dimensions, while words are used to uniquely name, describe and identify events, qualities or things. Mathematics is a language so unique to the mind that it can be used and understood by any foreign language. It is a kind of universal language that eventually rises in all other languages. It is a language within a language. Mathematics is communication by numbers. Language is communication by words.

Philosophers have long recognized that mathematics is a mental process that has meaning only to man. That numbers, like music, is an abstraction that has meaning only in the minds of humans. That the philosophers should fail to recognize language itself as an abstraction is tribute to its subtlety. Fire and the wheel have physical reality as objects. The words "fire" and "wheel" have physical reality as audible and visual (written) symbols up to and including the brain cells. Beyond that is the mind, where meaning is arbitrarily assigned and ALL is abstraction; not physically real.

For thousands of years men have twisted their minds dry, trying to understand the universe and man's place in it. None have had much success. The problem is not understanding the universe itself - it's man! Man doesn't appear to fit into a mechanical universe driven by the natural laws of cause and effect. Even when his logical mind can grudgingly agree that many of his bodily parts do function by the operation of known physical natural laws, he still takes refuge in those parts that retain some mystery, like the brain.

Another part of the problem of understanding is where does one begin the definitions? The solar system or just the Earth? The beginning of all life or just the beginning of mankind? All of these "beginnings" are shrouded in mystery and are theoretical at best. Should we be subjective or objective when trying to understand anything? All philosophers have warned that subjective views of the universe cannot succeed; the only logical way to proceed, in understanding anything, is to remove our own subjective thoughts, interests or feelings from the arena - be objective.

I cannot fault the philosophers' logic and they all wrote with admirable objectivity, as promised. But none succeeded in fitting man into the scheme of things! Perhaps the philosophers failed because they were wrong!

Perhaps there is no logically "objective" way to understand the universe and man - that the beginning and the end of time are so distant as to be subjectively meaningless. That only here and now and you and me, have all the meaning that can be understood!

The truth is, with all due respect, the universe before I was conceived and after I'm dead, means diddely-squat to me! I know that is a selfish, inconsiderate, utterly shameless and thoroughly frivolous point of view (and somewhat subjective), so call me shallow! But truth is what this little work is all about, and the truth is that man is intensely interested in how he, as an individual, relates to everything or anything. It is not the objective view, from the ivory tower of pristine mathematical logic that we seek. It is intensely personal.

The real beginning is where we, you and I, started our journey and I choose "you" as the "source" by right of poetic license. At the moment of conception you were only just that; a concept! The fertilized egg did not contain any cells or organs of your present body, only the genetic code of what might be; not what will be, but could be. The proviso "might be" is required because there are several trillion things that will affect the code translation through time.

While your growing body is in your mother's womb, it is very much a parasitic growth sucking nutrients from her body through the umbilical cord. Your mother's body is providing all the elements, proteins, liquids and gasses demanded by the growing embryo. When your body is born and the umbilical cord cut, the adult body is still only about 5% formed and "you" still do not exist. But the potential is there.

Over the next 3 to 4 years the brain will have completed its major interconnections, in the internal environment, and will begin to listen more and more closely to the signals from its external sensors. You begin to be aware of yourself and the world around you. "You" begin to form at the very centre of your body's sensory web. Somewhere within the internal darkness of the brain, connections are being made which relate various stimuli into patterns and things begin to take on abstract qualities, like good and bad.

You begin to equate things relative to your self. You are not aware that these qualities and relationships are being imposed on you by training, just as you are unaware that each of us is at the very centre of our own unique sensory view of the universe.

That is why "you" are the source! You are the source from which ALL understanding springs. You give substance, magnitude, direction and meaning to the universe. You are the one absolute in the determination of all things, great and small. From you all measurements are taken and all things referred.

You are the final arbiter of right and wrong, beauty and justice; but not truth, because truth is reality, not an abstraction. You will decide if what anyone has to say, in part or in whole, has relevance and meaning. You may, of course, shy away from this exalted position of determinacy, thinking others more worthy. Surely there are others, with years of professional training that are better equipped to make balanced judgments! There are an enormous number of professionals that would like you to think so. Modesty alone should give you pause. But don't judge too quickly, read on.

No new words or information will be used, but some concepts will be new to you and thus may sound odd or silly, such as "mind as the 5th dimension"; or "life as the 5th state of matter". All new words or ideas sound odd the first time we hear or read them. That's normal. But don't be afraid, they can't bite. The reason they may sound silly the first few times around is because they don't sit very well with the other "symbols" already in our memory banks. We can't "use" them; they don't "fit".

When a new word is presented it is expected to be first defined and then used in a phrase to make its meaning clear. An idea or concept may be expressed as a single audible (or written) symbol, such as "evolution" or "Bible", but a full description of either would take volumes. So it is with mind as the 5th dimension and life as the 5th state of matter; or the 1st and 2nd programs, (survival & reproduction), of all living things! These are what this little work is all about. They will be defined and used later. Right now, you're just getting familiar with the "sound" of them. (No, sound was not a misprint; trust me!)

You are also just getting familiar with the slightly odd concept of language as a stream of audible or written "symbols" that have been assigned arbitrary meaning. For example, we are communicating now by use of phonetic visual symbols! Sometimes referred to as writing or, in this particular case, printing.

This is only possible because we have both been trained to interpret certain visual symbols in a particular way; that is, reading and writing in English. It also implies a similarity of anatomical arrangement and function.

You, this page and the printing on it, both exist in a 4 dimensional space-time continuum called physical reality. This page and the printing on it also exist in the visual cortex of your brain; not as a tiny photograph, but as a small group of specifically activated cells. Your brain somehow interprets this chemical activity as a visual mental image - an abstraction. The physical page itself is scanned by your visual sensors which in turn are activated by light; electromagnetic waves. The printed letters are picked up as variations of frequency and intensity of that light. (Actually, you are not seeing the black letters, because they are absorbing light, not reflecting it. You are "seeing" the white page on which the letters are printed. If the page were black and the letters white, then you would "see" the letters - but that would look odd).

Each symbol (letter) has its own unique character, A, B, Z that is only recognized as a letter because your eye-brain has been trained to recognize it as such. That conditioning process was a long time ago, but perhaps you remember how difficult it was to memorize 26 letters. How you labored through the days, weeks and years, just learning to print letters and words. Each letter symbol is grouped with other letters to make a word symbol and as long as I continue to make word symbols we have both been conditioned to recognize, we can continue to "communicate".

8

By repetition, specific symbols are stored in the cells of the brain - remembered! We communicate through a chain of cause and effect physical events, which are expressed in standardized English symbols, to which our minds have assigned meaning. These symbols are meaningless to someone (or thing) not trained in their recognition and interpretation. They are abstract.

In man, the audible and visual symbols of language have evolved to facilitate communication at an incredible level of subtlety. The brain of mankind has become a symbol-cruncher of enormous capacity and flexibility. Consider all the world languages (about 5000) and the different audio, visual and even tactile (Braille) expressions of those languages;

Audio

- Speech
- Whistle signals
- Tongue clicks
- Alpine yodel
- African drums, etc.

Visual

- Writing (includes Cuneiform, Hieroglyphics, etc)
- Sign languages of the deaf
- Short hand
- Semaphore
- Smoke, etc.

All use various symbols which convey information between people trained in that mode of communication.

Language is the key that unlocks the brain and gives access to the mind; the place of dreams and imagination, the palace of reason with its dungeon of chaos.

In order to understand why we do the things we do and why we are here and what "it" all means, life and death and the journey in-between, we have to be aware of our environment. This is more than the world that surrounds our body, it includes our body. Our environment is everything, outside the conscious self, which affects "us". That means the entire universe and everything in it, from the beginning of time, including our own body.

To understand all of this is clearly impossible so we have to accept that full understanding is denied. We can, however, reach new levels of awareness by increasing the knowledge of how "we" interact with and interpret the external and internal components of the world. The external component is shared by all things. The internal component, your body, is exclusively yours. Because "you" can only view the external world through the chemical barriers of the sensors, we each will have a slightly different perception of it.

These small variations in sensorial acuity eventually add up to gross distortions of what "reality" means to each of us. There is only one external world yet many see a hell on Earth where others see a verdant paradise! Each separate understanding of the world is a direct result of the information, in whatever form, streaming into the brain via the sensory web. We will be taking a look at that web and at the stimuli that sets it trembling. I can't tell you everything you need to know because I don't know everything. You have to provide most of the information from your memory. Understanding will be limited principally by the amount of information you can acquire. It's not a gift - you have to work for it.

Let's start the journey by looking a bit closer at the concept of you as the **"Source"**. Did you ever consider the mathematical probability of your being here? That you might be the first true miracle you ever heard of!

The reason you may be a miracle is because of the high improbability of your ever being born! The odds against your birth are truly astronomical. Consider only the circumstances of your conception, for example. You are the product of the union of one of your father's sperm with one of your mother's eggs. Not just any of the billions of sperm your father was capable of producing, but "one" sperm - a particular sperm, part of the future you. Any other sperm would have contributed to a brother or a sister, not you.

You are from a "particular" sperm which united with one of the hundreds of eggs produced by your mother. Not just any egg, mind you, but a particular egg. Any other egg would have produced a brother or a sister, not you. Your brothers and sisters are from their own unique sperm/egg combination. That their bodies are separate and different from your body, in both time and space, is ample proof to the fact that each sperm/egg union produces a different offspring each time the same parents reproduce. So you see, you are from a particular combination of a specific sperm and a specific egg, and because of that particularity, you can never be duplicated - you are unique.

One sperm and one egg combination from about 4 billion sperm, times about 360 eggs, which were actually produced by your parents at ovulation time during their reproductive period; this does not include the billions of sperm and hundreds of eggs which, though available, were not used for procreation. The odds against your particular sperm/egg combination are already (360 eggs X 400 billion sperm = 144,000 billion) close to 150 trillion to one, and we're just getting started. Your particular sperm and your particular egg were carried separately by your mother and father who had to come together at a particular time and a particular place!

A mind boggling sequence of cause-effect events had to be orchestrated in time and through space, to bring them together at the precise instant your particular egg and your particular sperm became available for union. That your physical being is the result of the combination of a specific sperm with a specific egg is an axiom of the very highest order. Your spiritual self we can debate, but your physical body cannot logically be denied.

Women have 2 ovaries with approx. 400 thousand potential eggs, total. Of these, approx 360 will ripen and be dispensed in her reproductive life. The eggs are at different stages of growth. Several are ready in either ovary at ovulation time, once a month. The female will usually produce only one egg from the two ovaries but it cannot be predicted which cluster of eggs, on which ovary, will be the donor for that month. The eggs are distributed in the ovary and rise to the surface as they ripen; any one egg could begin to ripen. The egg and the sperm cell are specialized sex cells which each contain exactly half (23) the normal (46) chromosomal count of other cells of the body.

The male has two testicles, each generating billions of sperm over time. Sperm ready for use are stored and if not used are re-adsorbed and other fresh ones are delivered as replacements. At ejaculation both testicles contribute sperm to the seminal fluid and approx 100 million sperm are delivered into the female. The male and female human mate copiously but the majority of times there is no egg ready to be fertilized and the sperm are not used.

The sperm can survive only about 24 hours in the female and the egg must be fertilized before it reaches the womb. The egg reaches the womb by traveling down a fallopian tube, one from each ovary. There is only one period, of approx 48 hours, during each 28 days that the female is ready for fertilization. Thus, in any given month, tens of millions of sperm and one egg are lost. Only those sperm injected at or near ovulation stand any chance of fertilizing an egg. And that possibility is immediately cut by 50% because the egg must be fertilized before or shortly after entering one of the two fallopian tubes. Only those sperm which enter the "correct" oviduct can be successful. But they find the way heavy going because fine cilia, which line the oviduct, are sweeping against the sperm's direction of travel. The cilia are there to assist the egg's journey to the womb.

At the upper end of the oviduct, the ovary surface has already erupted an egg, which is drifting slowly toward the fern like mass that marks the fallopian tube's opening - from which sperm are already beginning to exit. The sperm surround and spread over the surface of the egg which though smaller than a pinhead, is gigantic to the microscopic sperm. Once any sperm has penetrated the egg's protein shell, and injected its contents, the egg is fertilized and a fast chemical change in the egg's protein shell blocks any further penetrations.

In fertilization, the 23 chromosomes of the sperm are added to the 23 chromosomes of the egg, thus making a total of 46 chromosomes, normal for all cells (except the sex cells) in the body. The chromosomes contain the hundreds of thousands of genes that are in turn the chemical coded instruction for the construction of your physical body. The fertilized egg continues on its journey to the womb, the life forces within it stirring up a small maelstrom of rapid cell division. Mathematically, your chance at life was so incredibly minute, and the dangers to its continuance so enormous, it's a miracle you ever got here. Congratulations!

This is, of course, not the whole story. We have only taken a brief look at some of the events associated with fertilization in humans. The surface of what is already known has barely been scratched. But one does not have to be a specialist to acquire understanding; only facts are needed and more facts tend to increase understanding. Just as you have your genesis in your parents, understanding has its genesis in facts.

Chapter 2

The Sensors: General

There are none so blind as those who will not look, and none so deaf as those who will not listen.

All sensory cells are configured by evolution to respond to particular stimuli. The word "configured" is used, in preference to "designed", because the latter suggests forethought, and no foresight existed or was needed for the evolution of any sensor - or any other organ or assemblage of organs (i.e. an animal). An organ is a group of specialized cells; an animal is a group of specialized organs.

The principle guide to a cells function and configuration was, and is, its utility to the organ itself and the animal as a whole. The template for its form was, and is, the natural physical laws in the press of necessity. Cell evolution continues today as it did 3 billion years ago. There is no magic or insight involved, just the operation of natural laws in circumstances current at a given time.

The sensor is real, the stimuli is real; the nerve fiber carries a physically real signal to a real cell nuclei in a real brain, made up of billions of other real cells - but the "perception" is abstract: does not exist in physical reality.

Although the sensors are configured to detect a given stimuli (light, pressure, etc.) it is the slight changes, with time, of some quality of the incoming signal that the sensor is actually responding to. A single photon does not a picture make or a single rarefaction a symphony.

All sensors convert their varied stimuli to one type of signal for transmission to the brain. The stimuli of light, sound, taste, smell, touch, balance, etc. are all changed into an ionic chemical wave, in separate nerve fibers that lead back to a particular neuron in the brain.

The sensory cell functions as both a detector and transducer of stimuli. That is, they convert the sensed variation of the particular stimuli to a common type of signal used by the brain cell. Although there is a voltage component to the nerve signal, the signal is not electrical conduction. The nerve fibers are long extensions of a neuron's cell wall and are electrically polarized; positively charged ions in the cytoplasm of the cell cause electrical potentials of approximately 50 to 80 millivolts between the fiber sheath and its contents. A flow of positive ions through a semi-permeable membrane in the sheath into the cell causes the sheath to depolarize. When the inside/outside voltage decreases to a threshold value, the cell fires an action potential which causes the local instability to be transferred into the immediately adjacent section of the fiber, which then repeats the action potential. The successive depolarization is an ionic transfer, with its associated potential difference, which sweeps as a single pulse along the nerve fiber.

The fact that the sensory cells are connected to nerve networks leading back to the brain creates the image that our body is physically wired. It is! There are nerve networks that run all the way from the brain to the little toe. On close inspection these are seen to be gross elongations of the wall of a single neuron in the brain or spine. At the little toe end, the fiber may appear to connect directly to a skin pressure-sensor bundle.

As our bodies are growing in our mother's womb, the sensory cells, nerve cells and brain cells are being formed. The wall of a nerve cell in the brain bulges its protein coat and slowly elongates one part of its cell wall toward a particular sensory cell. This elongation of the cell wall becomes an axon or nerve fiber, which contains cytoplasm continuous with the nerve cell nuclei. Specialized nerve cells may be interposed between brain and sensor to bridge the widening gap. The interconnections between the brain, nerve and sensory cell take place at an interface point called a synapse. There appear to be at least two types of synapses, electrical and chemical: electrical pass the ionic wave in either direction. The chemical synapse is one way only, and requires an intermediary, called a neurotransmitter, to get the signal across a tiny physical gap between the terminals of adjacent neurons.

After we are born, the nerve fibers continue to elongate as the body grows. The sensors detect various stimuli and send common message signals back to their specific brain cells, which are synaptically connected through ganglions (clusters of nerve cells) and more synapses to non-sensory cells. These non-sensory neurons interpret the signals into arbitrary abstract meaning in the mind. Only coded signals reach the brain. It is a place of eternal darkness and warm silence where rapid, tiny, chemical changes convey information between and inside single cells and groups of cells. We think of the brain as a single organ located in the skull, but it is actually diffused, by neuronal axons, through-out the entire body. Its cell nuclei are located principally in the skull and down the spinal column. Major motor control areas for the automatic operation of vital organs are often located in the primitive Spinal-brain.

I read a story once, of a decapitated chicken that survived for several days the sad loss of its head. The chicken was being processed in a packing plant when it managed to escape its tormentor just after the coup de grace.

Assuming it would soon die from loss of blood, no one bothered to chase it. At the end of the work day, it was seen to be still alive! A scab had sealed the neck wound and it was walking about, bumping into things. The work-shift whistle had ended the killing-day, so the chicken was left to its fate.

In the morning the chicken, sans head, was livelier than ever and the workers genuinely impressed. At lunch-time, since the chicken was still alive, it was decided to try feeding it to see how long it would live. It was captured and grain was pushed into its exposed, truncated, gullet.

I don't remember the chicken's ultimate fate; just that it survived the loss of its head, for many days, because the primitive brain in the spinal column was sufficient to provide basic motor-control to the legs and to the vital organs of heart and lungs. Gross but interesting.

The sensory cell is not a simple extension of the brain cell. Although all cells have essentially the same component parts, they vary enormously in size and function. Sensory cells differ as the stimuli to which they react; a light sensitive cell may be rod or cone shaped and a skin sensor may have a puffy button shape for pressure or a flat pad for heat (I don't remember which)- a taste bud is a group of sensory cells that looks like a lumpy mushroom. But all cells are separate entities. They inter-relate chemically with the fluids which surround them (for nutrient supply and waste removal) and communicate with their specific brain cell via a synapse - a small physical space between the sensory nerve fiber and the brain cell nerve fiber. Chemicals like acetylcholine, dopamine, serotonin, etc, called neurotransmitters, bridge the gap.

All sensory input signals to the brain must be learned. The taste, feel, odor, shape and color of an apple is different from any other thing, but these differences are all learned individually by separate sensors and only slowly come to be collectively identified with that particular fruit by the brain. It is the remembrance of these separate qualities that allows us to differentiate between an apple and a banana, using any one of the five senses.

If you where to slice an apple in half and then bite into a pear while holding the sliced apple close to the nose, the pear would "taste" like an apple! This is because the sense of smell dominates the sense of taste. We learn to associate small changes from our balance centre and a shifting visual scene with our body being moved though its surroundings. When we see an adjacent train moving slowly past us, there is momentary disorientation when it finally slides by and we see, by back-ground motion, that it is we who are moving. The sudden realization that it is we, and not the other train, that is moving is because our motion sensor in our inner ear had not responded to the smooth acceleration of our train. We thought we were stopped, and are startled to find ourselves in motion. The visual cues to motion are more sensitive than our acceleration sensor, so when we get a visual cue but no acceleration cue, we immediately assume that we are still and the scene is moving.

Because we sense no motion of the Earth, we automatically assume that the motion of the sun is real. It is no small intellectual achievement that allows us to accept that it is the earth's spinning about its axis, west to east, that causes the sun to appear to "rise" in the East and set in the West.

We have to learn and remember the particular audio symbol, as well as the particular visual stimuli, associated with the various colors. We do not automatically call a leaf "green" because we know it is green. Somebody named it green a long time ago and that name has been linked to that particular visual stimulus by the education we receive from our elders; as they were taught by their elders. Thus, if a person born blind due to physical abnormality has their vision medically enabled later in life, (a very rare and special circumstance), they do not immediately "see" if they have never seen before - they can't!

First of all, his eyes have to be able to track an object and the lens has to focus and the iris must adjust to light intensity. These are all learned subconsciously as reflex actions and are mainly automatic. Then he must learn as a child learns, as we have all learned; to relate vision with sound symbols (words). Even if he "knows" the difference between a block and a sphere by touch, he cannot "see" these word-identifiers in the objects themselves. He has to learn to associate an audible symbol with a visual perception. If allowed to handle the blocks he can immediately "feel" the shapes and thus identify them. If the objects were hidden from view for a while, he wouldn't remember, by sight, which was round and which was square. It takes repeated association to get any stimuli (information) into the memory banks; and that's just the start. There are literally millions of different shapes to be remembered and related. And if the shape is not remembered, as related to the word symbol, it cannot be recalled; even though we "know" the shape is in the memory bank! Quick now, what's a tetrahedron look like? What's the formula for finding the area of a circle? You were taught in school what an isosceles triangle is - can you still define or draw one. This is not an intelligence test but is meant to demonstrate that we often know considerably less than we think we know, simply because we cannot remember all we've been taught. But don't worry about it, the brain normally forgets any information that is not constantly used or re-enforced.

Visual recognition ability - seeing - is a learned, remembered function of the visual cortex of the brain. Vision is also remembered word-association with particular shape, size, color and movement: if it looks like a duck, walks like a duck and quacks like a duck, it probably is a duck. But you had to learn those relationships of the word (duck) with the vision (shape, size, color, etc.) and the sound (quack).

Learning to use our sensors is a life-long endeavor that is most intensive in childhood. As we grow and experience and remember, there is an imperceptible blending of the different senses that provide us with a smooth, seamless view of the world as a whole thing in itself. We are only intellectually aware of the blind spot in the visual field or the upper and lower limits of all our senses.

This is as it should be, because it gives us the feeling of security necessary for our physical and mental well being. But if you are to understand the world and your place in it, you must be aware that your sensors are responding to only a very small fraction of reality. It is intellectually chilling to realize that we are sensing far less than 1% of the natural world. The auxiliary units: radio telescopes, electron microscopes, CCDs, etc. used to extend the natural sensory limits, demonstrate the extreme minuteness of our normal sensory range. Getting to know the delicate sensory web is very important because ALL your information is transported by it.

The internal senses are not as easily identified to a specific sensory cell or organ, and the differences between a sense and an emotion begin to blur. Brain cell clusters have been associated, by probing, with centers of pain or pleasure, motor control, emotions, etc. but how, and from where, these centers are activated is not always clear.

That our internal sense of body-limb position is learned and grows with the body is brought into sharp focus by the experiences of amputees. The phantom limb syndrome is very real and scary. Where a limb no longer exists, the brain can still sense its shape, position and whether it's hot or cold - the limbs "presence" is still very real. Often a severe pain or burning sensation is experienced that can be cruelly disturbing mentally. The subject can clearly see that the limb is not there - it can't possibly hurt - but the pain can be very intense. In some cases, severing a nerve further back from the stump can help; if the doctor can find the right one to snip - unfortunately they are not color-coded, like the wiring in your T.V. set. A more typical complaint is that the missing part is in an awkward position or severely cramped. The missing limb's toes or fingers may "feel" painfully curled under or back and there is a constant reflex action of wanting to reach down and straighten them out. The conscious resistance to this learned, automatic reflex action is very exhausting because when they try any kind of diversion, the automatic reflex pulls the attention back to the pain - in a limb they know isn't there. What we all find odd, except the victim, is that the pain is real! With the obvious exception of local anesthetics (on a missing limb), ordinary pain-killers may relieve the pain. With time, the "phantom limb" may undergo uneven shrinkage. For example, in a leg amputated near the thigh, the foot of the phantom limb may still be perceived as full size, but now located near or inside the stump.

If you remember that our perception of body-part position is really just a complex extension of the brain cells, in so far as the senses are concerned, it begins to seem less odd. The brain has learned over many years precisely where each body part lies, relative to the adjacent body parts. It gets that information from an extended nerve network that may reach all the way down to the tip of the little toe. When that nerve path is stimulated, over any part of its length, the brain says "Hello, little toe; I know where you are!

The point to be noted is that the brain learns through the sensors where the body parts are, as a function of memory, and that the memory of our body changes slowly as we grow. The "memory" of a body part is learned as reality, by the brain. If the part is excised, the memory of it lives on in the brain.

One stimulus can sometimes appear to activate two different sensors. If we are blind-folded, on a bright sunny day, we have no trouble facing directly into the sun. Heat sensors in the skin pick-up the radiation and the brain is so finely tuned to its body envelope, that it can orient the body so that the area of maximum effect is located on the front of the head. In the totally blind, this sensitivity of the facial skin can often be used to locate a large, brightly lit surface.

A blind-folded person can detect the presence of a wall by echo-location. In a quiet room, the ears can come into use for large-object-location with just a little practice. As the blindfolded subject walks toward a wall, the subtle changes of sound reflection are well within the range of detection by the ear. For a sighted person, the "extra" sensory input from skin and ears is ignored in full light, but becomes slightly useful should the light fail. These little overlaps of stimuli and sensor are the cause of what is often referred to as a 6th sense. In the totally blind person, the "extra sensory" skin and auditory stimuli can be put to very good use by a brain struggling to orient the body to the physical world.

The five senses have been recognized for perhaps tens of thousands of years. The "sixth sense" has endured all through remembered past. It's that feeling that something just changed, ever so slightly, but we're not sure what. It is a convenient euphemism for an "odd feeling" we each get sometimes. Many "feelings" are in fact emotions, such as fear or hate; not a sense of fear or sense of hate. In order to qualify as a sense, there must be stimuli first and then a sensor to react to that stimuli.

There are literally thousands of potential stimuli for which we do not have a bodily sensor. We are only cognizant of them because of our intellectual ability to interpret their effects on the technological sensors - the devises constructed to interact with that part of nature beyond or dangerous to our natural sensors. The body is unaware of the radio and TV (microwaves) passing through - but the radio and TV receiver tells us the electromagnetic energy is there. Thousands of neutrinos from the sun pass through us each second, with no detection and very little damage. Hundreds of cosmic rays, powerful beta particles and background atomic radiation and magnetic fields waft through the body undetected; and with incidental cellular effects that we hope are minor. Various types of radiation detectors can betray their presence. We cannot sense minor voltage differences, but if the voltage is high enough to breakdown the skin resistance, the current-flow can be sensed as pain. Best to check for voltages with a voltmeter.

One may be quite unaware that a burglar has passed through their home while out walking the dog - but the dog will know. His nose can track the exact path of the intruder, hours and even days after the event. If you have some understanding of canine behavior, you will then also know your castle has been violated. If you're the average person, you'll just think the dog's excited to be home.

The reason vision is discussed at greater length than any other sense is because we are more aware of it, and thus have investigated it more, than the other senses. This gives the illusion that it is superior to all other senses. It is not. We are simply more conscious of visual perception because it requires more voluntary control of the body than any other sense. The only way we can see something, within the field of vision, is to consciously open the eye-lids and "look" at it. The aperture control is handled by sub-conscious learned conditioning of the reflex-arc, between the photo receptors in the retina and the brains evaluation of the total light intensity, followed by the brain's controlled adjustment of iris muscle-tension for optimum light-level. But the focusing mechanism is under voluntary control, to allow for your selection of depth within the visual field. Most adults have no problem with deliberately de-focusing the lens of the eye, but it does take some practice to consciously override the auto controls normally in effect, we cannot over-ride the iris auto control. We must also voluntarily re-position the eyes in their sockets, in order to locate the item of interest onto the fovea (where we see detail) of the retina. Maintaining binocular vision requires an incredibly sensitive discrimination of separate control signals to the six major muscle groups for each eyeball. Each eye requires a slightly different orientation within its eye-socket, in order to keep its fovea on the central visual axis. A few individuals can put a voluntary, full control, over-ride on these positioning muscles; all of us can deliberately "cross" our eyes. The only way we can see something not in our field of vision is to deliberately reposition the head and/or body, so that the object is within about 80 degrees of arc through 360 degrees around a line perpendicular and central to, a line connecting the pupil of each eye.

Such elaborate voluntary organ and body orientation is not required for the general, everyday, use of any other sense. It is that required-voluntary-control that holds our attention and prompts us to give vision the regal status of King of the Senses.

Without the sense of pain, one would have to be very careful as to where the limbs were at all times, and very cautious about touching anything that might be too sharp, too hot, or too cold. An ordinary hot cup of coffee could be very dangerous. Without a pain sense, you could seriously scald lips, mouth and throat and end up in hospital on a respirator while you recovered. Although it's a rare occurrence, some have been born without this valuable sense. Those that manage to make it to adult-hood are covered with scars and often crippled. Even the innocent act of sitting in one position too long, crushes motor-control nerves and restricts blood circulation to the limbs. Sleeping requires soft wrist restraints, to prevent the sleeping body from rolling onto an arm and cutting off circulation to the hand. A life of continuous pain is as sad as a life with no pain - a mix of both (light on the pain, please) is required.

There are about 150,000 cold sensors and about 15,000 heat sensors spread throughout the surface skin. Millions of pain sensors are located throughout the body.

Taste and smell could be dispensed with, if you could stand a world without chocolate ice-cream and the scent of roses. It is the protection provided by community living that allows one to think that only the quality of life would be diminished with their loss. You cannot go to the grocery store and buy a product, whose taste or odor will kill you, which is not clearly marked as to the danger. There are severe penalties for anyone foolish enough to sell you poisonous or spoiled food stuffs. Even so, it sometimes happens, and that is when one's lowly taste buds and olfactory organs come to the rescue. The sour milk, rancid butter or moldy bread rarely leave their wrappings before being angrily deposited back on the grocer's counter with demands for refund.

The survival value of the taste and odor senses are diminished in modern society, but their acuity can be revived, should society ever fail. Primitive man depended on these two senses in the selection of what was good to eat - and what was bad. Given the perceived threats to civilization, that seem to grow more ominous each day, one might be well advised to hold onto taste and smell for a while longer; they might come in handy yet.

Although we are aware of hundreds of different tastes, the experts say these are all variations on the four basic perceptions of salty, sweet, sour and bitter.

To be without the sense of hearing would be a great loss, but again, most would say if they had to choose between vision and hearing, that vision would get first place. I have read articles that place vision as the primary sense because it accounts for 80% of mans knowledge, through the process of reading, (the percentage varies with the article, but they all claim over 60%). I guess they forget that writing is done with a "phonetic" alphabet or perhaps those articles were written when Hieroglyphics were in vogue. The fact is, because we do have phonetic writing, audible-word-symbols obviously came before visual-written-symbols! If it were not for audible symbols, mankind would not even exist because spoken language is the basis for thought itself. Without audible language there could be no phonetic alphabet and I could not write, nor you read, this or any other book.

To be born with any single sense not operating is a sad loss. But the brain is quite unaware, and the individual quite undisturbed by its absence, initially. I must emphasize that I'm not referring to multiple dysfunctions which often include a sensory loss - I refer only to a single, total loss of one sense. With this in mind, the loss at birth of the sense of hearing will have far reaching effects that only become apparent when the child begins to interact with other persons, and is an almost insurmountable barrier to formal education.

The blind brain and the deaf brain begin building their sensory web before birth and after birth there is a fantastic rush to get the interconnections in place and begin the job of coordinating organ interaction and sensory information with muscle response. Both brains are totally unaware of their deficiency, but while the blind mind is receiving the occasional odd message, via the ear, in reference to something called "sight", the deaf mind "sees" nothing odd. He sees people facing each other, moving their lips and hands. To him this is not odd; they have always done that - its normal activity! When he tries to do it, they get angry and he can't understand why. Because his brain has never experienced sound, he doesn't know that this activity is called "talking" and involves "sound". When he tries to join in with this activity, he's unaware that his exaggerated facial movements and arm gestures are viewed as some kind of gross convulsion by those around him. His only motive is to join in on this normal activity - to belong. But the harder he tries, the more firm the rebuff. His rejection is a complete mystery to him and is devastating emotionally.

His mind becomes very busy with other matters. Unfortunately, his custodians have just missed the point at which he was most ready for contact - about one year old. As growth continues the blind mind is absorbing all kinds of information, in the form of language, while the deaf brain languishes in the flood of visual and tactile stimuli that conveys little information and NO understanding. The deaf were at one time, often misdiagnosed as idiots.

The blind mind, through language, begins to associate feelings such as "hunger" and "thirst", with the words "food" and "drink", but the deaf brain can't. It has no "word" for the feeling and no "word" for its relief; the fragile, unused motor-control links to the mouth and larynx begin to fail one by one. The brain has to be made aware of its deficiency as soon as possible - one, because it will be many years before it can begin to appreciate its impairment and - two, because if the communication areas of the brain are left idle beyond 2 years old, their critical interconnections will begin to fail and intellectual capacity will be reduced forever.

The difficulties of contacting and educating the deaf brain serve to highlight the utility of language. It pulls ALL sensory input, internal and external, into a single unified field of consciousness. It makes thinking practical and the expression of the inner-self possible. If one can begin to understand the significance of hearing-loss to the individual, it is easier to understand, that in mankind as a whole, if the sense of hearing (and speech) had not developed, audible language would be impossible. Without language as a base, none of the institutions of our societies could exist - civilization would not exist - mankind would not exist.

Language is the great unifier of the different interpretations our brain associates with the varied stimuli it gets from its two environments, external and internal. The reactions to signals originating from the external environment (usually considered physical and beyond our skin), we call **"sensory" responses**; such as vision, hearing, taste, etc. The responses our brain gives to the varied stimuli originating from the internal environment (usually considered chemical and from the skin inward), we call **"feeling"**

responses; such as hunger, thirst, waste elimination (need to go to the bathroom), tiredness, hot or cold, etc.

Another level of sensory awareness is that associated with what we call **emotional responses** of love, hate, fear, happiness, sadness, anxiety, etc. These "emotions" are the brains evaluation of the bodies (brain included) chemical balance. Psychiatrists will often prescribe mood-altering drugs to help a patient "feel" better. Addicts use drugs to get high and feel better.

Senses are our brain's perception (psychological response) of stimuli from our external environment. Emotions are our brain's perception of stimuli from our internal environment. The area common to both sensory and emotional perception is the conscious brain. It has access to an aural linguistic code that applies a remembered audio symbol (word) to the stimuli that caused the response. But that remembered audio symbol was invented by mankind and had to be "learned" by the brain using it, as associated with a particular stimuli = perception response.

Because ALL our internal responses are ultimately chemical in nature, we have no way of knowing which particular hormone triggers what emotional response; happy, fear, love, etc... Although the studies of how certain mood altering drugs (opium etc.) that stimulate specific cells in the brain have lead to the discovery of endorphin hormones produced naturally by the body under stress, there is still much to be learned about how we "feel" happy or sad, love or anger. The emotional centers and sensory centers are all located in the brain - in the head. Not in the heart or chest as the ancient ones believed.

Language is the common factor in all things "sensed", whether physical or emotional (chemical, which itself is physical at the atomic and molecular level!). The hundreds of different senses are each given a "word-tag" and it is the word-tag sound that the brain uses to inter-relate the thousands of different impressions. The brain "thinks" with the word-tags that it has learned represent "things" as diverse as; real - abstract, solid - gas, hot - cold, happy - sad. Words are used to link all the various sensory responses into a common pattern (sound) that allows the brain to think. Thinking is done with the audible symbol (word) that represents something (hate, hunger, pain, tree, and book) rather than the thing itself. All words are real whether spoken as an audible pattern, written as a visual pattern, or thought as a neuronal pattern.

The things that sound-symbols represent may be real, as a violin or the sound it produces; or abstract – "music" if the violin sounds are pleasant, "noise" if they are not. But the "meaning" of all words is abstract even if the thing represented (a house, say) is real. It is the "meaning" assigned to the word-sound that is arbitrary and abstract, not the word-sound itself.

The point of understanding about our external sensory web is that it detects "information", in all its varied forms, from the physical world around our bodies; the external environment. At or near the body surface, ALL the various types of mechanical stimuli are converted to a single type of ionic chemical waves (chemical re-actions are merely electromagnetic phenomena at the atomic and molecular level - still mechanical), for transmission in the internal environment of the body. All external and some internal (balance etc.) information is transmitted directly to the brain via separate nerve fibers and is consciously knowable or acknowledged. All of this information is used to keep functionally aware of our environment, moment to moment, while we are awake. Ninety-nine point ninety-nine percent of this information is immediately forgotten because it has served its purpose of orientation, and is no longer needed. Only that portion of information above the arbitrarily set awareness-level of each sense is held briefly in the brains short-term memory banks. Among the point 01 percent of information coming in that is used briefly, is that associated with the hearing organ or seeing organ and that we understand as language. Audible language memory allows the brain to assign identifier symbols to every thing it consciously senses and thus gives rise to awareness and mind. Everything that the MIND of man knows or can know has its base in the information transmitted to the memory of the brain, by its external and internal sensors.

Upside Down or Downside Up

A filmed record of an experiment by behavioral scientists was made in the first decades of the 20th century in Scotland (Glasgow University, I think). In the 1960's it was dusted off, re-examined, and parts of it shown to the public because of its novelty.

A man was equipped with a set of special glasses that fitted snugly to his head and caused his visual field to be inverted. The purpose was to learn if the body could adjust its coordinated activities to a world that now appeared to be upside down. The glasses would only be removed, in the dark, for sleeping. Some of the filmed experiments were quite funny to watch, which accounted for the public interest.

On the first day, the subject was seen to have some difficulty walking on uneven ground or going up or down stairs. Opening a door required great concentration to connect hand with door-latch. When a glass of water was offered at chest level, he reached a foot or so lower to grasp it. A playful "sword-fight", with toy sabers, showed him totally incapable of warding-off even slowly delivered blows; a parry to the head produced the response of shielding the groin; a poke to-ward the stomach caused the subject to protect his face. It was all in good humor and the slightly accelerated motion of the early cinematic product made it all quite humorous.

By the end of the first day the subject was just barely able to walk about the campus, unaided - running was dangerous - self feeding was slow and required considerable effort to get food to stay on a spoon long enough to get the spoon into the mouth, instead of on the nose or chin. Reading and writing were impractical. The simplest tasks had become extremely difficult or impossible. Even recognizing close friends wasn't easy.

By the end of the third day he was able to function without assistance - walking was almost normal and running possible. Reaction was still slow but now fairly well coordinated to the proper response. By the end of the first week he was practicing riding his bicycle on campus and his physical actions and responses near normal - reading and writing still very difficult.

By the end of the 2nd week he was riding his bicycle through town traffic and was fully independent. By the end of the 3rd week he was having little trouble with any task, even reading and writing was close to normal. So the glasses were removed!

The physical tests, done at the beginning of the experiment, were repeated on the subject with the same humorous results - but reversed this time. When the glass of water was offered, he reached a foot above it! A playful poke at the groin caused him to shield his face - he had difficulty recognizing close friends. Walking was difficult and he could not climb or descend stairs safely, without assistance. It all looked even funnier now; because without the glasses there was no clue as to why this man had such odd responses to ordinary events!

By the end of the day the subject was worried, and the controllers concerned because the disorientation was as severe as the 1st day of the experiment. This was not expected and they had stopped laughing! They had assumed that the experiment would be over when the glasses where removed; but it wasn't! They had seen no danger in the experiment to the voluntary subject, because round-the-clock attendants had been provided for his safety and if anything went wrong, the glasses could be removed instantly by the subject himself.

They had all expected considerable disorientation, at first use of the glasses, and they where not disappointed. They had all expected the subject to eventually adapt to his inverted vision, and again they were not disappointed. What they had not expected was that the "normal" responses of the subject, learned and re-enforced over years of time, where now gone. Wiped out in only three weeks of inverted visual stimuli!

The subject was seen to be pitifully disoriented and the only quick cure was to put the glasses back on. It was belatedly recognized that the recovery of the subject was going to take a few days, at least. The surprise was that the complete recovery-adaptation was only a day or two shorter than the original sensory accommodation! Conditioned reflexes, which had been learned in childhood and re-enforced over years of normal sensory adaptation were not indelibly imprinted into the voluntary motor-control areas of the brain; they could be "forgotten" in a matter of weeks!

There had been some hints that what we take as normal activity is in fact a conditioned reflex, which if not used is lost. Use it or loose it, says the physiotherapist (and the sex therapist too!). A patient that requires several weeks of bed-rest has to "learn" to use their legs again.

Permanent loss of a sensory ability is nicely demonstrated by some cave animals. Some fish and insects have been trapped in total darkness for many generations and the eyes of these animals are not only completely insensitive to light, but the body has begun to slowly withdraw the energy requirements needed to produce these now useless organs. Loss of the faculty of vision, if not stimulated shortly after birth, can be easily demonstrated in any animal, including man. Animals blind-folded from birth, will be unable to form a visual image when the blind-fold is removed at adolescence.

They may be light sensitive but can never learn to "see". Because the brain was not stimulated to form the delicate interconnections of cells in the visual cortex, at the allotted time-interval of genetically controlled growth, the intricate co-ordination of eye control (focusing, adjusting light intensity, coordinated eyeball positioning, etc.) with brain cell activation in cortex and motor-control areas, cannot take place. Once the biological time slot for the programming of a sensory perception has passed, without stimulation, that sense can never be fully awakened.

An animal born with a correctable defect to the eye (cataract) or ear (canal blockage) will be severely impaired for life if the fault is not corrected within a few months of birth. The stories of adults suddenly being able to see or hear are just that, stories. These faculties may be "restored" to the adult who has had their use interrupted by some accident. But it is a sad truth that something that never was, will never be. We cannot restore something that never was, and we can only acquire sensory awareness during the period of biological growth set aside for its introduction to the growing brain.

The Sense of Vision

The eye is not just a light sensor - it is a whole multifunction organ that: focuses light, adjusts to light intensity, rotates in its socket, has a built in "jitter", is constantly scanning the field-of-view, and has a miniature chemical laboratory to keep the rods and cones of the retina light-sensitive. Only the rods and cones are photo receptors, the rest of the organ supports and promotes that function. Auxiliary eyelids and tear ducts protect and lubricate its delicate exposed surface, and it is recessed into a bony socket to give some mechanical protection. Muscles attached to the eyeball provide for synchronized movement within the eye sockets.

Light from the scene being viewed is focused as a real image, upside down, on the retina. This light must pass through both a layer of optic nerve fiber, and a web of blood-vessels feeding the retina, in order to reach the light sensitive rods and cones. And just to make things even more difficult, the rods and cones appear to face the wrong way - they point toward the pigment layer at the back of the eye. The retina appears to have evolved backwards! The optic nerve bundle exits the rear of the eye through the visual field and thus produces a blind spot in each eye.

A small depression in the retina, called the fovea, is axially centered and is the place of most acute vision. It, and a tiny area surrounding - called the macula, or yellow spot - is densely populated with light-sensitive cells, and the overlay of blood-vessels and nerve fibers is minimal here. The cone cells predominate in the fovea and are thought to be the color sensors. The rod cells are more numerous in the rest of the retina surrounding the macula, and are thought to be insensitive to color. The rod cells are more sensitive to light intensity than the cone cells. Color disappears in moonlight but one can still see quite well, thanks to the rods.

If you're trying to see something on a dark night, try looking slightly to one side of the object and it will appear a bit brighter. This is due to the object of interest being located to just one side of the fovea, where there are more rod cells. You sacrifice detail, but the method might disclose a tree stump instead of a bear.

The cone cells are color sensitive to red and green in a small central area, and this small area plus a small border, is also sensitive to blue and yellow. This color sensitivity appears to be due to genetically determined pigments in the cone cells, which explains how red-green color blindness can be inherited. Fortunately, the light-sensitivity of the cells is typically unaffected but the individual sees red or green as various shades of yellow. In any case, vision - color or black and white - takes place in the visual cortex of the brain. The eye, elaborate as it is, is a light sensor only; it does not "see".

Although the whole scene being viewed is in focus over the entire retina, one can only see fine detail in that part of the image that overlays the fovea. This is an extremely small area (about 1%) of the total visual field. The human eyes are therefore constantly darting from point to point, to get a detailed look at the whole picture. We are not normally aware that detail can be seen only in the direct centre of where we look. For example, look directly at any word in the centre of this page, and without moving your eye, try reading the print an inch or so on either side.

If one keeps the head still, and just moves the eyes, you can consciously scan your eyes over any part of the visual field, without the field itself moving! Move the head slightly, and the visual field changes. Hold the eyes steady on something and again move the head, the visual field shifts. So long as the head is not moved, the visual field stays rock-steady, while the eyes bob about to pick up detail; something like the "highlight spot" that TV programs use to pinpoint a particular face in a crowd.

It is the brain that is holding the visual field rock-steady, in its short-term memory banks, while the eyeball rolls the fovea of the retina back and forth over the tiny inverted image, so you can make out detail. The brain is doing it right now - in the visual cortex - at the back of your head!

This amazing ability of locking the visual field to head orientation gives one the odd feeling that the brain is actually looking at the world through the eye sockets of the skull. The visual field is only that part of the world that can be seen when the eye sockets are turned toward it. If the head is tilted from side to side, the field remains steady and horizontal; just as if it were a picture hanging on a wall!

When you consider that the tiny image projected onto the retina is now tilted, with respect to the eyes horizontal axis, and thus overlaying a changed set of photo-receptors, vision becomes even more amazing; the visual field really is tilted on the retina but the brain is able, by coordination with other sensors, to say it's the head that's tilted, not the field. Knowing that the brain has made a correct judgment is far from understanding how it did it.

Even if the eyes are deliberately held focused on one spot, there is still a tiny "jiggle" to the eyeball that is easily seen by your physician, but not by you. The purpose of the jiggle is probably to prevent a continuous exposure of constant light to an individual light-sensitive cell, because once the cell has "fired", in response to a light photon, it cannot fire again until re-energized; and it cannot be re-energized in full light. Each scene viewed is normally composed of light and dark areas, so the normal jumping around of the eye to pick-up detail, causes any given cell to be constantly exposed to varying levels of light and dark. A thin wash of visual purple from the pigment layer re-sensitizes receptor cells in those brief moments of reduced light.

Visual purple is a compound of vitamin "A" and protein. Lack of vitamin "A" in the diet can lead to a visual defect known as night blindness; the individual is totally blind in dim light due to a loss in sensitivity of the retina of the eye. This is particularly sad for very young children, because if not corrected, permanent blindness will develop due to the brains loss of stimulation during its critical learning period. Much blindness in poor countries is simply due to the lack of vitamin "A" in their meager diet as children.

Looking at a bright light or exposure to a bright flash, will leave the eye with black spots in the visual field; or if the eyelids are closed, bright spots. They are black with the eyes open because the small groups of cells overlaid by the bright light source are de-sensitized, relative to the rest of the cone/rod cells; bright with eyes closed because they are still firing, while their neighbors are shut-down due to lack of stimuli. This slow decay of sensor cell activity, after the stimuli is removed, is called persistence. It is exploited by movies and TV to give us the illusion of motion through rapid exposure of still-pictures that vary sequentially from exposure to exposure.

The reason then, for structuring the retina backward, to the direction of travel of the light photons, is so that the light - sensitive cells may be constantly re-sensitized by fluids from the pigment layer. If the rod/cone cells were facing forward and in front of the blood-vessel/nerve-fiber network, we would have a clear view, but only one look, because without visual purple to re-sensitize the cells, they could only "fire" once. This understanding of "reverse configuration" helps in the appreciation of just how incredibly gossamer the retina must be, in order to pass the maximum light consistent with structural stability.

The nerve fibers from each small group of rod and cone cells in the retina of each eye are brought back to the brain in a most peculiar way. First of all, all the nerve fibers exit as one bundle, from the back of each eye. These two bundles then unite into a common sheath just below the brain's two frontal lobes; then the common sheath separates into two separate bundles again. Each of which then ends up, eventually, in the left and right visual cortex at the back of the brain.

Now imagine a vertical line through the center of the visual field of each eye - the left side of each eye goes to the left side of the brain while the right side of each eye goes to the right side of the brain! Considering that the image on the retina is inverted to begin with, and the retina is installed backward, the "wiring" seems to be inordinately complex.

The optical nerves home in on a lower mid-brain area called the right and left Lateral Geniculations. From here the signals are passed through synapse and ganglia to reach the cells of the visual cortex where "perception" begins to take place. How the brain can form a single , apparent, full color three dimensional image, from two eyes (and then hold it steady while the eyes scan it), from chemical blips inside the head, and make us believe the scene is outside the body (where it actually is), remains one of the wonderful processes still waiting discovery. It is a remarkable achievement.

The normal human eye forms clear images from infinity to about twenty-feet at rest. Closer than that requires some use of a Ciliary muscle to change the lens' curvature and thus re-focus a clear image on the retina. Two forward facing eyes provide man with binocular stereoscopic vision; good for judging distance and precision in hand-eye co-ordination. Part of the reason for the diverse nerve route from eye to cortex may be because some body responses must be activated before the mind is conscious of a perceptual image.

Any object detected as fast-moving and close to the delicate sensory organ demands the fastest possible defense reaction. The eyelid slams shut and our head is already moving, to avoid the missile, before we are conscious of the threat. This is a learned reflex action and is made possible by the ganglions (groups of nerve cell nuclei), which allow the interconnections to voluntary motor-control sections be short-circuited into automatic motor-control sections, for very brief periods.

This interrelated system is partially pre-connected by inheritance, but must be activated into action, and extension, by practice. It must be exercised and becomes sluggish if not worked. The "blink" defense is expressed within a few weeks of birth but other defenses, related to head-dodging and whole body movement, must wait for neural and muscle development still to come.

The variety of light-sensitive cells plus the variation in organs making use of these cells has produced an enormous number of different eye types. The camera type eye has evolved with mammals (including man) and mollusks (octopus) but there are many other types of "eyes" in use. Each animal species seems to have come up with its own version of the ideal photo receptor. The variation in design and configuration seem to be endless. Even the simple and compound eyes of crustaceans (crabs, clams) seem to grow more complex the longer we examine them.

The reason for this is twofold, one: any cell or organ is an evolutionary compromise between the cell/organ, the animal, and the internal/external environment, and two: our own sensory range is being continuously extended by machines and techniques that allow us to see more clearly into the structure and operation of cells.

That all of these visual organs should be responding to one small section of the electromagnetic spectrum (less than a full octave wide), that happens to be co-incident with the centre of the solar spectrum (as seen through earth's atmosphere) is no accident. The visible wavelengths are between about 400 and 700 nanometers and that is where the interaction of light energy with electrons first becomes significant. Longer wavelengths (infrared) just bump the atoms and molecules around and thus are usually sensed as heat. Shorter wavelengths (ultraviolet) have too much energy and can knock an electron clear out of its atom.

This ionization can permanently damage a molecule (which is an assemblage of atoms) and is thus threatening to a living cell. In the narrow energy gap between too much (ultraviolet) and too little (infrared) lies the just-right area, where the energy of the electromagnetic spectrum (the part we call "light") is in tune with the electronic harmony of chemical activity. Here, the energy of a given wavelength can make or break the valance bonds of molecular structure and thus influence (cause, if you like!) a specific chemical compound (protein!) to come together or separate.

For the purpose of detection, all that is required is a change and a measured response to that change. The retina of the eye responds to changes in light frequency and intensity - nerve fibers carry the measured response into the visual cortex - the brain "learns" to interpret various "light" patterns as vision.

The visual mental image itself is an abstraction – it is a "pattern" of activated brain neurons - doesn't exist in reality.

Because perception takes place inside the brain, it is a very personal experience. We learn to see, and because there are thousands of physical variables associated with the process, we cannot say for certain that any of us end up with the same visual information when we all look at the same thing. Different eyewitness accounts of a single crime are often completely at odds with each other. This is usually NOT due to a fault in the physical detection system (eyes - optic nerve - visual cortex), but to the interpretive part of the brain that tries to make "sense" of the incoming stimuli.

Most of you have been exposed to visual illusions where the scene remains unchanged but the mind can flip back and forth between two interpretations! The black and white illusion of the vase or two faces is a common one. At first sight, it may look like a white vase on a black background; the next instant, it can be two black silhouettes of heads facing each other, against a white back-ground. The apparent change is not taking place in the picture or the eye; but in the brain. The sense of vision is a process of sensory input AND intellectual assessment. The eye only detects the electromagnetic waves. The brain has the perception of "light" patterns (vision) and interprets it as best it can, by comparing it to past experience - it is a learning process.

The person who says they can remember the room of their birth and the Doctor's moustache are deluding themselves. The sense of vision could not be activated inside a coal-black womb! At birth, the retina may be slightly light-sensitive (for a purpose other than vision) but the rest of the eye-organ is quite untrained in its multiple, coordinated functions necessary to form an image on it. The eyelid itself is involuntarily closed for the first few days; the brain is much too busy controlling basic life functions (in a suddenly alien environment) to be bothered with trivial visual or auditory stimuli.

Although it is impossible to be certain about what another animal "sees", it can sometimes be helpful in understanding human vision to compare our eye with other animal eyes. Most dogs have an extra eyelid, located under the more common upper and lower eyelids. Called the nictitating membrane, it is a third eyelid of vertebrates and more common in reptiles and birds than mammals. It can be moved, like a vertical sheet across the eye, from the inside edge to the outside edge of the eyeball. It's pale white and translucent; assists in keeping the eye clean and is often deployed while the dog is under water. The dog's eye is similar to the humans in structure, but the retina has no fovea, and only rods, no cones, for light sensors; this suggests that dogs cannot see color or detail. Behavioral tests indicate color-blindness and low sensitivity to the shape of an object; the dog's eye could not see the detail needed to read a book. It does respond very well to motion. A dog's visual field may appear in its brain as a gray sheet, where only relative motion, not the edges of things, is detected. When looking at the forest, in still air, there may be a simple uniform field of gray; no trees, rocks or grass would be seen. The slightest movement of a leaf or blade of grass however, might show up as a black shape, in an otherwise featureless scene.

To be able to ignore all stationary objects and see only movement would be a very handy trait for a hunter! As soon as the dog begins to move, the relative movement of nearby bushes and rocks would make them stand out against the back-ground. Next time your out with the dog, try standing perfectly still and down-wind. If he's tied to a post and watching you and you don't move a muscle, not even your eyes, the dog may get quite excited because you have just disappeared! He may begin to tilt his head from side to side or jump about, to create the relative movement that will get you back into his picture of the world. But one has to be very still, because the dog's visual field will instantly respond to the slightest motion.

At night, if you shine a flash-light at a dog, you may notice the beady little red spots in the centre of each eye. This is light reflecting off the retina in back of the eye, and coming back out through the pupil. Its redness is due to pigment at the back of the eye, but may also indicate that his eye is sensitive to infrared light; he may be able to see a "hot" ground-hog moving against a "cool" earth back ground.

Not all fish can see color but salmon and gold-fish can. Fish-eyes do not have eyelids and the lens is moved back and forth (rather than changes in curvature) for focusing; their bulging, side-mounting provides a 360 degree visual field enveloping their body- they are the center of a visual bubble.

Eagles and high-flying hawks have the sharpest acuity of all eyes, because their retinas have the highest density of photo receptors - in full color (we think). They can spot a resting mouse where we could barely make out a cat.

A mountain goat's eye has a horizontal slit-type iris, and the retina has a macula arranged as a faint yellow horizontal band. If the goat could read, it suggests he could stand in front of a wide shelf of books, and read all the titles without moving his eyes - visual detail is not limited to a single small spot (as in the human eye) but is laid out in a continuous band clear across the visual field. Very useful for rapid travel across cliff faces.

House-cats have a vertical slit for their iris. It is believed that this allows them to see above and below the visual field normal for a round pupil, without moving the eye. Handy when catching birds!

Most carnivorous and omnivorous animals have forward facing, stereoscopic, binocular vision (like man). It is the specialized sight required in hunting other animals for food. Most herbivorous animals have developed large, protruding eyes, with little or no overlap of the visual field of each eye. They can see front, back, and side-ways all at once; it's called keeping an eye on the carnivore.

Compound eyes are the many faceted eyes of insects and crustaceans. The outer surface is covered with hundreds or thousands of lenses and each lens is located on a tube with one or more photo receptors at the bottom. It is believed that no visual image is generated in the brain - strictly a motion and light intensity detector. Simple but effective - ever try to catch a fly! Bees and many other insects can see into the ultraviolet - helps with flower selection. The eyes of lobsters and some bivalves have reflective membranes and may incorporate light guides, cylindrical lenses and parabolic mirrors in their structure; a compound eye may have fewer moving parts but can be much more complex than the camera type, in the manner in which it processes the electromagnetic waves. There are many, many kinds of eyes, and each has its own little story to tell.

COLOR TV OR BLACK AND WHITE!

On a Fall Saturday morning I was discussing, with the wife, the practicality of replacing the old black and white TV with a color set. Color sets had been long in the market and their price had fallen to be within reach of our meager savings (we could afford the down-payment). Our two sons were watching cartoons on the TV. They were about 6 and 4 at the time, and the eldest said, "What do you mean, Dad, color TV?"

I was surprised for a second and replied as to what I took to be obvious. "Well, ah. This set has a black and white picture." "No it doesn't!" they both chimed.

I pointed at the set and said, "This is a black and white picture, it has no color!" "Yes it does," both chorused again. I was more surprised then ever!

"Do you mean to tell me you can see color in this black and white picture." (I double checked it to be sure.) "YES!" they both agreed. "You're sure?" I couldn't think of anything else to say. "Yes, it's in color," they both agreed again.

I was at a loss for words for at least a minute. Stunned into silence, I couldn't help grinning at my own confusion as I tried to figure a way out. The old man was trapped, at last, without an answer. I stared at the black and white picture of Donald Duck in a boat, and in a flash of genius, asked; poking at the set, "OK, what color is the water?" "Blue!" They both answered.

Trapped again. After all, water is usually colored blue! "OK, what color is the tree in the back-ground?" And immediately bit my lip.

"Green!" They both answered, with a giggle at pop's dumbness. Trapped again. Trees are green! I couldn't help laughing out loud because there seemed to be no way out of this puzzle.

"OK, wait a minute, le'me think." I continued watching the picture. "OK, if you guys are so smart, what color is Donald's jacket?"

And I smiled with satisfaction when they couldn't say for sure. It was many years before I realized that during that brief moment, in three separate brains, the ratchet-wheel of knowledge advanced by one tooth and the pawl of awareness dropped snugly into a new slot.

A different understanding for each. For my sons, the mind would slowly stop adding pigment to their cartoons and they would soon see only black and white, where once they saw glorious color. Because there was no visual sensory cue for the brain to whip out its paint-brush, it had to be the MIND that was providing the illusion of color from remembered past experience. Some might regard this faculty of the mind as a benefit, and mourn its loss.

But is illusion more beautiful than truth? If you think so, you're going to be very disappointed with this book!

For me, it was a quick peek into another dimension. Today, I wonder how much of "reality" is illusion or delusion. If one could remove the rose (or grey) colored glasses for a clear view of reality, would one have the courage to do so?

The Sense of Hearing

The sense of "sound" is in the brains interpretation of the messages sent to it, via nerve fibers, from the sensory organ; in this case, the ear. Like the eye, the ear is an organ of multiple parts whose configuration is arranged to promote and deliver the physical stimuli to the sensory cells. The stimulus which activates this sensor is physical vibration of the medium (gas or liquid) in which the animal is normally located. In the case of man it is small compressions and rarefactions of air, caused by some distant air disturbance, which pulses information to the ear drum.

The information is contained in both amplitude and frequency of the vibrations and is mechanically transferred to the sensor/transducer in the inner ear. Here, mechanical vibrations are detected and converted into an ionic chemical wave in nerve fibers leading to the auditory centers of the brain. The brain then learns to interpret these physical stimuli as a "sense of hearing" that we call sound. Unlike the eye, the ear is so blatantly mechanical in operation, there is little difficulty in understanding how it functions - until the vibrations reach the inner ear.

Although all senses are equally important for maintenance of the body in its environment, hearing takes on particular significance for humans because it allows the individual to experience mental interaction via language. But the organ looks like something assembled by a child or as if nature were trying to imitate a machine. It's a Rube Goldberg design that had Edison or Bell presented it to the patent office, they'd have been laughed out of the building.

It begins with a skin covered flap of cartilage (the Pinna) mounted on the side of the head, called the ear. Its' smoothly curving contours direct air vibrations into the outer ear canal. The canal passes through the skull and is completely closed by an ear-drum (Tympanum) about three-quarter inch inside the head. Past the ear-drum is the region of the middle ear, where three tiny bones (the hammer, anvil and stirrup) create a bridge from the ear-drum to another diaphragm, behind which lies the vestibule of the inner ear and a small spiral tube (called the Cochlea). Inside the cochlea, on the floor of the tube and stretching deep into the spiral, is a furry layer of fine cilia, immersed in a fluid that fills the cochlea. This is believed to be the sensory detector (the Organ of Corti) that responds to vibrations of the ear-drum, which are carried by the three bony Ossicles to the fluid in the Cochlea. The outer ear directs compression and rarefaction onto the ear-drum which converts these pressure variations into mechanical motion. The Ossicles transport this mechanical motion into the fluid of the cochlea. The fluid transports these vibrations to the cilia which are thought to be part of the sensory cell. The Organ of Corti then converts the frequency and amplitude of the complex mechanical vibrations into ionic chemical waves that travel up nerve fibers into auditory brain cells which give birth to the perception of "sound". Sound is an abstraction - it is a "pattern" of activated brain neurons - does not exist outside the animal brain.

The Inner Ear Labyrinth

The central portion of the labyrinth, called the vestibule, is where the snail-like coil of the organ of hearing connects to the fluid-filled semicircular canals that form the organs for detecting rotation in the three planes of space. In the vestibule itself the Utricle and Saccule, which aid in our sense of balance and are sensitive to gravity pull and lateral acceleration (elevator and automobile). The entire labyrinth is filled with watery fluid.

The different mechanical sensors responding to gravity, rotation, acceleration and sound are essentially all specialized organs of touch. The utricle senses gravity as a pull on tiny grains of calcium carbonate attached to cilia extensions of sensory cells. At the enlarged ends of the semicircular canals, mats of cilia extending from sensory cells detect relative motions caused by head movement and fluid inertia.

The Organ of Corti, which senses sound vibration, is a mat of fine cilia extending from sensory cells and immersed in Endolymph fluid. The base membrane of the Organ of Corti is about 32 mm long and follows the two and a half turns of the Cochlea. It is about .05 mm wide where it attaches to the vestibular wall between the oval and round windows, and about .5 mm wide at its end, just before reaching the apex of the coil. High frequencies (20 kHz) are detected at the vestibule end - lowest frequency at the apex.

All sensory cells require nerve cells to carry their messages to control centers. A typical neuron consists of a cell body that contains the nucleus and other organelles that serve to maintain functions vital to its survival and operation. Extensions of the cells membrane make up its maze of thousands of branching dendrites, which receive stimuli from other neurons or sensory cells. An enlarged extension of the cell membrane becomes an axon or nerve fiber. Absent in some small nerve cells of the cerebral cortex, the axon is what we usually think of as the peripheral nerves that thread throughout the body. These axons are usually covered in a fatty-white sheath called myelin that specializes it for rapid transmission of simple, all-or-nothing, ionic chemical impulses. At the end of the axon are the many splayed ends of effector terminals which form synapses with other nerves or muscle tissue. These splayed ends are also called end-brushes and secrete the various neuro-transmitter chemicals needed to pass the nerve signal through the synapse junctions and thus activate some other cell or a whole chain of cells in a reflex-arc. Some myelinated nerves can conduct at about 200 meters per sec., while small non-myelinated fibers in the autonomic system conduct at about one meter per sec.

The auditory nerves conduct at about 25 meters per sec. and are myelinated. Recovery period after conduction is one to three milliseconds and a neurons activity is measured in number of impulses per second. Maximum frequency of impulses is about 1000 per sec for the first two or three impulses, but that falls rapidly to an average maximum rate of 200 or 300 pulses per sec. The only significant gradation of pulses is; one, the number of pulses per second; and two, the time (or phase) relations between impulses in the same fiber and in neighboring fibers.

So how does a frequency of five thousand or ten thousand cycles get detected and transmitted if the average maximum frequency of nerve pulses is only three hundred per second? The same problem of comprehension occurs again and again where ever stimuli are encoded for transmission to the brain. How does light or touch or taste reach the brain? Maybe a closer look at sound-wave detection can help clarify things.

The Cochlea, Fig. 1, is the hardest bone in the body and the Ossicles of the middle ear are the smallest bones of the body. The Cochlea is fitted inside with what amounts to three fluid-filled tubes.

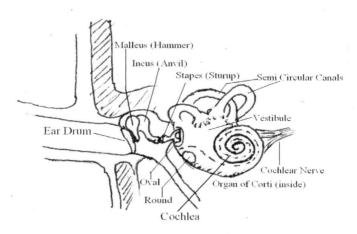

Fig.1 The Inner Ear Labyrinth

The Organ of Corti, Fig, 2 and 3, plus the other sensory cells in the vestibule are all in one tube assembly filled with the watery fluid, Endolymph. The other tubes complete the packing of the bony Cochlea and are filled with Perilymph, very similar to fluid in the spinal column and brain. The three bones of the middle ear transfer vibrations from the pearly-gray ear-drum to the oval window membrane in the Vestibule. Two tiny muscles, one to the Malleus (hammer) and one to the Stapes (Stirrup) pull in opposition to provide dampening at high sound levels to protect the sensors from amplitude overload while improving frequency response.

Length of fibers increase progressively between the two windows to the Cochlear Apex.
Fig.2 The Basilar Membrane, (Plane View), & rows of hair cells, 1 inner, 3 outer.

When the Stapes (stirrup) is pressed against the oval window it forces against the Perilymph fluid in the Vestibule. Because fluids are basically not compressible and the Cochlea bone is immovable, the Perilymph is displaced into the stretched membrane of the round window, which can move into the air of the inner ear. Because the Scala Media Tube, containing the Basilar Membrane, Fig. 3, is part of a flexible partition between the fluid filled chambers fronted by the oval and round windows, the Basilar Membrane is subjected to the displacement movements of the Cochlea fluids.

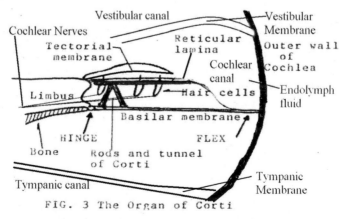

FIG. 3 The Organ of Corti

At above sixty-cycles per second the inertia of the fluid and the flexibility of the Basilar Membrane are such that there is no fluid flow around the center of the helix, where the two chambers, Scala Vestibuli and

Scala Tympani, become one. Under vibrational impact the Stapes presses in and out, the fluid, Organ of Corti and round window all displace in step with the Stapes and fluid flow by-pass is minimal, Fig. 4.

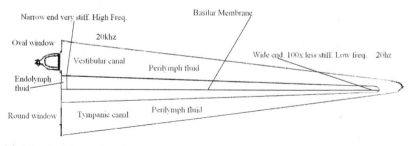

Fig.4 A mechanical view of how the Basilar Membrane relates to the Cochlear Horn, (Coil straightened out). The coil is as important as the horns internal shape when considering reflected waves reinforcing standing waves in the membrane.

The individual nerves do not fire at the frequency of the received sound. The conical and spiral shape of the Cochlea plus the variable stiffness, width, length of the Organ of Corti are the frequency selective agents, while fluid is the carrier of physical vibration. When a frequency is impressed on the Cochlea a standing wave is created some place along, the 32 mm of Basilar membrane, as determined by; the inertia of the fluid, the stiffness of the Basilar Membrane, the cross-sectional area of the Cochlea and the curvature of the spiral; - here the Basilar Membrane has its maximum amplitude of distortion.

The membrane does not actually vibrate - it distorts. The location along the membrane is sensed as frequency and the amount of distortion is sensed as amplitude or loudness. This distortion causes the Tectorial Membrane to slide slightly relative to the Basilar Membrane containing the hair cells, Fig. 3. Because the hairs, as many as 80 per cell and only seen by the electron-microscope, project into the Tectorial Gelatin, they are moved back and forth relative to the cell body. It is believed this sub-microscopic movement stimulates the hair cell to signal its several afferent, (sensory), nerves to fire their train of action potentials up the axons (nerve fibers) toward the brain. A single frequency is rarely encountered in the normal environment. Typically a range of frequencies and amplitudes is being received non-stop 24 hours a day; even while you are asleep and not "listening". Thus the Basilar Membrane is in constant microscopic motion.

As seen edge-on, the membrane distortions with frequency and amplitude would appear as tiny traveling waves sweeping back and forth along the length of the Organ of Corti. At any given instant the position along the membrane of any distortions marks the frequencies being detected, while the degree of physical distortion is the measure of amplitude, or loudness, of those frequencies.

Increasing the amplitude (not the frequency) of the physical stimuli increases the rate of nerve impulses. Thus the rate of nerve impulses is the measure of loudness, not frequency. Frequency is determined by "position" along the length of the Organ of Corti of the sensory cell being activated. The hair cells are not resonating to a particular frequency.

All sensory / nerve cell combinations have essentially the same output regardless of the nature of the stimuli, i.e., all-or-nothing. The level at which an action potential takes place may be raised or lowered by the central nervous system.

Efferent, (motor), nerves from the brain also connect up with sensory nerve dendrites near the hair cell bodies and they can enhance or inhibit the afferent (sensory) nerve action potential. It is these efferent nerves that are allowing us to select or "listen" for a particular sound in a broad range of simultaneous sounds. Similar types of efferent control of sensitivity or action potential are characteristic of other sensory and motor control systems, including the retina of the eye.

The Cochlea and the Organ of Corti have converted mechanical vibration into nerve impulses on specific nerve fibers, but there is still no "sound". The afferent Cochlear auditory nerves home on a small area of the brains Cerebral Cortex, called the Primary Auditory Center. One on each hemisphere, shared by each ear. It is here in the cortex that mechanical and chemical activity finally becomes the psychological phenomena of "sound".

The number of afferent nerve fibers from the Organ of Corti is about double the 12 thousand hair cells and there are about 500 efferent fibers coming from the brain. There are about 350 sensory cells per millimeter of Basilar Membrane. Each afferent nerve may be activated by 3 or 4 hair cells and each hair cell may be reached by 2 or 3 nerve cells. This overlap provides some redundancy for death or malfunction of either a hair-sensory cell or its message nerve path to the brain.

All information to the brain is coded information. Sensory and nerve cells do not conduct the stimuli they receive. They can not conduct electromagnetic waves of light or mechanical waves of vibration. These are stimuli only. The sensor responds to the stimuli and detects the changes in those stimuli. The detected changes are chemically relayed - transduced - to specialized nerve cells that carry the measured change in physical stimuli as the pulses of an ionic chemical wave toward the brain.

The brain only gets nerve impulses, nothing more. Brain "location" determines the psychological sense or emotion. It equates frequency of nerve impulses and number of nerves activated with amplitude of detected stimuli, nothing more. We "learn" to distinguish one frequency from another in the same way we learn to distinguish the "quality" of a musical note - middle "C" as sounded by a piano, a trumpet, or a violin - by practice. We learn to hear and then to listen, just as we learn to see and then to look - by practice and repetition. Sensory acuity is not automatic - it must be learned.

All vertebrates below the mammals have simpler organs of hearing. In the mammals, the middle ear cavity and its contents (Ossicles), is derived from the Pharynx and connected to it by the Eustachian tube; one from each middle ear leads back to the Pharynx and permits atmospheric pressure equilibrium to be maintained across the ear-drum. None of the animals below the fishes seems to have developed an organ for detecting vibrations, though all fish and a few amphibians have evolved a row of pressure sensors, located in the lateral line.

This lateral line stretches from head to tail along each side of the body and is believed to aid the fish by sensing slight water pressure variations, and possibly very low frequency vibrations; created as water moves around objects or as objects move through the water, as well as depth information. Water is a very poor conductor of sound energy because the great mass of water molecules quickly absorbs the energy of vibration. And because the absorption varies directly with frequency, only very low frequencies, better described as tactile pressure-waves, can travel any appreciable distance.

Vertebrate embryology shows that the three tiny bones of the middle ear have their origins in the gill structures of our aquatic ancestors. In the early stages of a mammal's embryonic growth, transitory gill slits can be seen to form in the proximity of the Pharynx, in the area to become the neck. These do not develop into true gills. The tiny cartilage supports of the first pair of Pharyngeal Pouches can be seen to migrate from the Pharynx into what will become the three bones of the middle ear. Note that this is the same area of the vocal cords! This may mean that some speech center cells associated with the Larynx (organ of sound production) are being stimulated by the auditory processes or vise versa even though both structures are well separated in the head location. This may have been a critical factor in the development of "language", as opposed to the relatively simplistic ability of "hearing" or "sounding" as separate, non-related functions. The Tonsils, the Parathyroid and Thymus glands derive from the second, third and fourth pairs of the Pharyngeal Pouches.

The human ear normally responds to vibrations between frequencies of 20 to 20,000 cycles per sec, which we perceive as sound. Many animals detect higher frequencies and some, like bats and dolphins, are well known for their use of high frequency sound in echo-location; as an aid in hunting and avoiding obstacles in total darkness. This secondary use of hearing (echo-location, not just listening) is only possible where the animal has developed a method of providing its own controlled sound source. An object is located by the hunter producing its own high frequency sounds and listening for the reflections of that sound. In the case of the use of "sound" for under-water echo-location, it should be kept in mind that vibrations travel very poorly in open water - and the higher the frequency the shorter the distance traveled. The "sound" that these aquatic creatures make is in fact a series of very sharp clicks. Our ear interprets a stream of these sharp clicks as a sound sensation, but the Dolphins or Beluga Whales are not generating these clicks as a sine wave but as very sharp peaks of pressure. It is these pressure peaks that travel through the water at speeds and distances forbidden to vibrational waves, that the animal (all Marine Mammals, by the way) is making use of. For large object location, a low 200 clicks per sec would sound a bit like a 200 cycle hum. For small object location, or for detection of more detail, a higher 2000 clicks per second would sound like a whistle. These clicks are not generated by the external blow hole (which the animals can use to generate air vibrations) but by some method inside the head. The fine oil in the heads of these animals is believed to act as the concentrator, director and transfer-medium required to get the pressure waves into the water. The Beluga Whale in particular has considerable muscle control of the oil sack mounted on the front of its skull.

The third use of sound, social communication - language, appears to have arisen only in some mammals and birds. It is dependent on the animal's ability to produce sustained, controlled vibrations in the air or water. The principal and original benefit of detecting vibrations in the environment was its survival value. It helped first, to locate the individual within its environment and second, in avoiding or locating something that caused vibrations. Sound helped the hunter find its prey and helped the prey avoid the hunter. Thus there was, and still is, a double-positive bias for natural selection to favor the more sensitive ear for survival and reproduction in all animals.

Sound symbols then, as best exemplified by man with his gift of speech and invention of language, have become the most powerful vector in the natural selection of any species on earth.

The question of whether mans gift of speech is due to neuron interconnection between the speech center and auditory center (i.e. internal) or in a reflex arc via the middle ear to those same brain locations (external) is not idle curiosity. As you come to understand what language means, you will appreciate that if the loop is all in the brain, then any animal with more than three different sensory cells may develop a mental code - a language. If an external reflex arc is required, then only some mammals will be able to serendipitously stumble on an auditory code of language.

Only mammals have utilized obsolete parts of the pharynx to construct a section of their hearing organ. Ancestral nerves from the ear drum or from the ossicle muscles could provide the feed-back to the speech center. If language does require an external reflex arc, then man is even more unique than he ever dreamed possible. I remember reading somewhere that when a speakers' voice is tape recorded and the output of the recorded words are played back by earphones to the speakers' ears, with a delay of about 135 milliseconds, that the individual has great difficulty in continuing to speak!

Pavlovs' Dogs and Conditioned Response.

Ivan Petrovich Pavlov was a physiologist doing experiments with animals in the early 1900s. They were designed to prove a theory he had about the bodies' reflex actions. He was trying to prove that reflexes were learned, involuntary responses to stimuli, and that they could involve secretory glands as well as muscles.

He called the results of his experiments "conditioned responses", but could just as well have used the term, the death of free-will, considering the flak he took from colleagues. The only reason his theory became so well known to the general public was due to the gross vulgarity of the photographic proofs that finally silenced the un-believers. The photo story, of conditioned response, appeared in magazines of the late 1940s or early 1950s and was a sensation because it horrified the public; not the theory, the photographs!

The animal experiments were simple and direct. A dog was fed immediately after a bell was rung. The dog was in a comfortable cage and could poke its head out through a hole to feed. Fastened to the side of its jaw was a small tube that was connected to a salivary gland. A small bottle could be connected to the tube for measuring the quantity of saliva produced. After several days of bell ringing, followed by food, it could be clearly seen that the salivary gland was producing its secretion in preparation for eating.

Now, the bell would be rung but no food would be given. Again, the salivary gland could be seen to secrete, with no food within smelling distance - The salivary gland was being controlled by the sound of a bell! Normally, one would have expected the salivary gland would be activated by the smell, taste or sight of food; and it is. One would not expect the salivary gland to be activated by stimuli, like sound or light, which has nothing to do with food; but it can;

Before the conditioning, the bell is rung and it can be seen that no saliva is produced. After the conditioning which allows the dog's brain to learn to associate a sound with food, the gland secretes (and the stomach secretes) in response to the sound alone. A response that is normally and naturally activated by food is now activated by sound. Not a "natural" response but a "conditioned" response; a conditioned reflex of the salivary gland and its tiny muscles to the sound of a bell.

Because the external conditioning stimuli cannot be associated with the biological utility of the reflex (i.e. there is no point in salivating if no food or drink is about to pass into the stomach.), it meant that any conditioner could be used in place of a bell; a gong, a light, an electric shock, a chemical smell or taste, a physical slap to the body or even a word. Any word sound, that the animal could recognize, could be used to produce a conditioned response. And that the conditioner was in fact a "cause" of the "effect", that Pavlov called a conditioned response.

The implications of a causative relationship as opposed to an intellectually purposeful relationship, between the world and the body of an animal (man) were seen as a threat to free-will by a few. For some strange reason they felt that playing a piano or working a typewriter was some kind of gift from a higher power - that a skill had nothing to do with the hours, days and years of practice, that went into the skill's expression!

Many objections and criticisms were offered by the few, and each was laid to rest over years of now frustrating experimental variations. One objection was very difficult to counter - that the signal controlling the salivary gland was from the gut and thus could not be "learned". The solution was something never tried before, and the pictures of its' rendering jolted minds around the world.

A conditioned dog's head was severed from its body and another dog's functioning blood system was diverted to include the severed head, to keep its brain "alive". In the photos, the head was shown on a platter and its tongue was seen to be touching its lip, where a drop of weak acid had been applied as a stimuli. The story continued to say that, yes indeed, the salivary glands did secrete, at the sound of a bell, in the severed head of a dog that had been trained to the conditioned response. There was no response from the doubters.

Free-will loosed its white-knuckled grip on the body of man and scuttled further back into the mind; where it thought it was safe.

Chapter 3

Language: Its True Value To Mankind

In the beginning was the word. Speech is a biological gift to Homo Sapiens. The ability to make controlled sound (speech) was with man long before language made its appearance. All humans have the gift of speech and no primitive tribe has been found to be without language. Language is an invention of each tribal group. It is so common and fundamental to our every day existence that, like gravity or the air we breathe, we rarely give it a second thought. It is as easy as seeing or walking. We only appreciate the complexity of language when we try, as adults, to learn a foreign tongue. Talking in our own language is so easy that many do it without even thinking! The last sentence should bring a snicker because of its absurdity - to talk, one must think - talking is thinking. **Language IS thinking.**

Language is composed of symbols - audible and visual symbols. Our forbearers of a million or so years ago were unaware of the intricate interconnection of ear-brain-throat that made audible symbol communication (language) possible. Speech was available for use, so man used it in his own small groups, quite unaware that he was "inventing" anything. Each separate group came up with a different language because they could assign any meaning they wanted to any particular sound. It is that assignment of a particular meaning to a particular sound symbol that has significance for man: it gives physical reality to abstractions.

Language is to the brain what binary code is to the computer; it is the carrier of information, in a sequence of discrete symbols, arbitrarily assigned abstract meaning. Arbitrary assignment of meaning meant that speech could be used as a means to represent "something", like Mom or Dad. Not just for mimicking the sounds of animals while on the hunt or for pleasure, but to make a specific sound symbol to be assigned whatever meaning was needed. In the processes of evolution, language has become the finest sieve used by nature to separate the wheat from the chaff of humanity.

The controlled generation of sound in vertebrates is commonly associated with the trachea of the respiratory system. Frogs (amphibia) have a Larynx with vocal cords but lizards and snakes (reptiles) do not; nor do fish, crustaceans or insects. Only mammals and birds have evolved an elaborate, finely controlled, "sounding box".

In birds it is called the Syrinx and is a chamber located at the junction of the lower end of the trachea, where the two major bronchi branch into the lungs. Here, a flexible membrane can be projected into, and vibrated by, the air stream from the lungs. Muscles control the membrane tension and thus can vary the pitch of the sounds produced. Some "talking" birds can mimic human word-sounds very clearly; some, such as the Mocking bird, imitate other bird calls.

In mammals the voice box is called the larynx. It is located at the upper end of the trachea and is most highly developed in humans. From the pharynx, that short section of throat between tongue-root and Adam's apple, a slit-like opening - called the glottis - leads into the larynx. This opening is flanked by cartilage and by muscular folds, the vocal cords, embedded in the mucous lining. The larynx is further supported by large right and left plates of cartilage in a "V" shape - the Adam's apple. When not in use, the glottis opening is a wide "V" shape; when sounding, throat muscles pull the ligaments of the vocal cords taut and the glottis becomes a mere slit, vibrating in the expelled air from the lungs.

Because the pharynx is a passage common to both trachea (breathing) and esophagus (eating, drinking), a flap-like epiglottis closes down over the glottis during the act of swallowing, to keep food and drink out of the lungs.

The human voice apparatus involves not just the larynx but the whole front of the head, most of the mouth and throat, and the lungs and diaphragm. Speech begins with an intake of air into the lungs by a contraction of the muscles of the diaphragm; followed by a muscular contraction of the vocal cords in the larynx. This creates a narrow slot, with the vocal cords across the upper end of the trachea. The diaphragm, in controlled relaxation, allows the lungs to collapse, thus forcing air through the vocal cord slit, causing them to vibrate rapidly. The frequency of vibration is fundamentally determined by their thickness and length; they are controlled by the tension of muscle fibers. Small people generally have higher pitched voices than large people, because the vocal cord mass is smaller. The larynx, containing the vocal cords, produces sound and can vary in pitch while sounding. The combination of air flow and flapping vocal cords produce sound waves of compression and rarefaction in the airways of pharynx, mouth and nasal passages. These add qualities to the basic tone that helps make your voice sound different from others. As the modified sound passes through the mouth; tongue, pallet, teeth and lips all conspire to form the raw sound-wave into controlled, audible sounds, called speech. With practice, the individual can slowly learn to consciously control the various muscles of diaphragm, larynx, tongue, lips and jaw to form very specific sounds that duplicate the "word" sounds heard by the ear.

There are about a hundred different sounds that can be shaped by the human vocal tract, called phonemes, that are used singly and in combination to make up words. But any one language uses only a small fraction of the total - English uses about 40 phonemes, the alphabet being 26 of the most common ones.

We have to stop talking in order to breathe. It is possible to speak while inhaling, but it does take some practice so most people don't bother. A child will occasionally speak on the intake but adults rarely get that excited about what they have to say. We also have to stop talking (and breathing) while eating or drinking because, as adults, we have a short passage of throat that is common to both eating and breathing. This isn't true for newborn babies. For a few weeks after birth, a human baby's feeding and breathing systems are separate; part of the reason babies have practically no neck. He can suckle at the breast for as long as he likes, breathing all the while through the nose. In a few weeks he'll have to pause for breathe, because the genetic code controlling growth is making changes to the throat. The pharynx is elongating to include both eating and breathing - getting the voice box ready.

Two of the first sounds, produced by trained conditioned response of the English child, are "Momma" and "Dada". It is the child's first "rite of passage" into the English speaking culture and the first introduction, to the brain, of an arbitrary assignment of an audible symbol to a visible object. Within a year, that brain will fuse that sound (word) and that vision (momma) into a single concept in the mind - the audible symbol and the visual object will become one and the same. This fusing of a word identifier to a thing or event or idea continues throughout life but is particularly intense during formal education. We do not think of this as conditioned response training but that is precisely what it is. We are trained to associate a particular word (sound symbol) to a particular thing or meaning. Nothing wrong with that! That is how language is learned. But I hope you can see that much mischief can be done to a child during the learning phase, by an educational system that is cognizant of what it is doing!

The Cardinal who said to his Pope, "give me a child before he is seven and I will give you a Catholic for life", knew what he was talking about. The important thing to keep in mind is that language is "arbitrary" and it is "learned".

Because language is arbitrary, the meaning assigned to each vocal sound (word) will vary between isolated groups such that each group will develop its own unique tongue. Because language is learned, word definitions will vary slightly from individual to individual within each group. This variability in definition of a word (sound symbol) goes a long way in helping to understand why it is that there is so much confusion and disagreement between people that have a common language!

For example, I was very fortunate in having a Mommy and Daddy that did not abuse me. You may not have been so lucky. The "meaning" of these word identifiers (mommy and daddy) might be significantly different for you and me. We might only agree on their biological definitions. A quick look in any desk dictionary will demonstrate that any given sound symbol (word) can have a great many different, and even unrelated, definitions as to meaning. So, saying what you mean and meaning what you say can often be extremely difficult.

In fact, one would expect that such variations in understanding of meaning should lead to considerable confusion; diverging and even opposite conclusions from the same knowledge-base. And it has! Mankind has no agreement in deities, politics, beauty or justice. There is as much difference of opinion between members of a linguistic group as between the diverse language groups themselves. Language gives expression to reason, as well as to chaos, in both the individual and the group. Understanding the seat of chaos is a major theme of this work - which we'll get to later.

That language is an invention is evident from the great diversity of languages in use today. About 3000 separate languages world-wide are the distillates of tens of thousands of languages that evolved over the past hundreds of thousands of years. The human communications system of ear, brain, and speech-generator, are essentially identical in each individual, but each separate group has given its own sound symbol to represent a particular thing. The children of these groups then learn those audio symbols by conditioned response. We all grow up with the mistaken belief that a given audio symbol is the same as the thing itself. It is only as we gain experience that we can begin to understand that the word sounds would have either no meaning or some other interpretation to another language group. That to us, trained in English, all other languages are gibberish. The reverse is also true - our language, English, is gibberish to anyone trained in foreign audio symbol representations!

There are no classrooms in any language group to instruct the children in the first use of audible symbol communication. Each child must learn the subtleties of sound interpretation (listening) and audible symbol reproduction (speaking) without formal instruction. It is an intellectual achievement of the very highest order. That such a task should be set before a six month old child can be vaguely appreciated by those adults who have tried to learn a foreign tongue.

The learning process for understanding language starts the moment the brain begins to receive the auditory sensations from the ear - before the ear has "heard" a single word. The ear, like all other surface sensory organs, is both a detector of stimuli, and a transducer to convert the detected change to a nerve impulse. Only the coded nerve impulses reach a particular part of the brain that interprets those pulses as "sound". After birth, it takes several months of monitoring the various senses, and the flood of information carried by each, before the brain begins to get things sorted out. As the brain slowly learns to coordinate sensory function with various stimuli, the eye-brain begins to watch and the ear-brain begins to listen. The relationship between sound waves heard by the ear and sound source, as indicated by visual tracking, blends into a deepening understanding by the brain. (Ever notice how a nine month old child will strive to locate visually, a sound source!) Audio symbols (words) are beginning to be associated with "sounds", which are in turn being associated with the movement of the mouth parts of Mommy and Daddy.

In the beginning, the "words" we hear are just audible symbols - they have no meaning - just sounds that people make. The brain manages to hold onto some of them because they are repeated over and over again in natural speech. The brain begins to remember the most repeated sounds and the "patterns" in those sounds. Identifying body parts with audible symbols is another clear indication the brain gets of audible symbol equals "thing" relationship. The audible symbol that expresses "nose" becomes identified with the physical object, nose. It becomes the "word" for nose. Once the child begins to talk, the search for word identifiers (audible symbols) becomes intense - it wants to know the "word" for everything in sight.

A symbol can be used to represent something - anything. A flag is a visual symbol that represents a country; all large companies develop a graphic sign or logo that is used to "symbolize" a particular company. As children, our custodians assign us each a sound symbol that becomes our name. The behavioral modifiers of "yes" and "no" usually come immediately after the name identifier has been implanted. Spoken language is a sound or group of sounds which are used as audible symbols (words) to represent some physical thing (a man) or abstract idea (Sherlock Holmes). We make up the assignment of words. We decide what words will mean. Languages are not gifts or discoveries, but inventions! Inventions of the MIND, spoken by the mouth, heard by the ear, mediated by the brain. Audible symbols given abstract meaning!

Audible symbols, words, language is baffle-garbage to those who have not "learned" its use. The acid test, of the utility of language in the process of thought, is to try and "think" in a foreign language! Try to think of water, or anything else, in Arabic or Inuit, for example. You might rightfully point out that it is silly to even try because you know nothing about these languages. But that is precisely the point I'm making; we cannot think in their language any more than they can think in English! Without remembered audible symbols (language) to interconnect the different perceptions being detected by the various sensory organs, we cannot think. These audible symbols are the base on which all other methods of communication (visual, tactile, and auditory codes) are based. Memory can yield-up the separate tactile, auditory, and visual impressions of tossing a stone into a quiet pond (feeling the stone, hearing the plunk, seeing the ripples) but only language can tie these perceptions into a time-dependent, conceptually-whole experience, that I can "think" about and express to you - by using words.

I cannot think of "water" in any language but English. I cannot think in any language but English. It therefore appeals to me as being reasonable that without some form of audible (or visual or tactile) symbols, the brain cannot think: And if I cannot think than "I", the inner me, cannot be. My physical body (including the brain mass) would still be here, but the concept of self would be gone without words to give it substance!

We are poised on the edge of a mental "black hole". If language is essential to the awareness of "self" (I can't think without it) and language is composed of words (symbols) to which our minds have arbitrarily assigned meaning (and we know this to be true), that suggests that everything is an invention of our own mind!

You are the source, what do you think? Are "you" a figment of your own imagination! DON'T PANIC - all will be explained later. But please, give it some serious thought and hold onto your sense of humor - it might come in handy.

Whether or not you can bring "yourself" to believe in the internal implications of language, I'm sure we can agree that language is essential for external communications. Without language we could not express our thoughts, let alone "ourselves". Without language to convey meaning we could understand little.

The ongoing attempts of technology to reproduce or synthesize - as opposed to simply recording - the human voice, or to develop a machine for speech recognition, is helping to clarify just how complex spoken language is. When reading a book we can clearly see the divisions between words and sentences by the use of blank spaces, capital letters and punctuation. But the spoken language is a continuous stream of sound, generated by the vocal cords and modulated by the mouth parts. There are few pauses between words or sentences; an articulate speaker will usually pause only briefly for a breath! Relative to other English-speaking peoples, we all talk with some kind of accent or word-emphasis peculiar to our local group. Irish, Scot, British, American, Australian accents do not impede understanding provided local vernaculars are avoided. When conversing in a crowded, noisy bar, we have no problem selecting the voice we wish to listen to from the babble of voices in the room. This is because the ear-brain can consciously "listen" for a particular amplitude, frequency or pattern within its spectrum of "sounds"; while simultaneously ignoring louder sounds not related to speech. Oddly, this ability is lost if the sound waves are mechanically reproduced by a hearing-aid or tape-recorder! In English, because the pitch, or frequency, of the voice is used principally for emphasis of words and to indicate sentence-stops, we can whisper our words without loss of meaning. But we cannot whisper a tune, because the meaning of music is partly in its pitch and tone, which are only expressed by changes in frequency. Some foreign language words have their meaning in pitch; that is, the same phoneme given in two different frequencies will have two different meanings. Which is why some Chinese phrases cannot be meaningfully expressed when whispered; nor can some of the "click" or "cluck" sounds of some African languages. Deliberate tone inflection in English speech is often reserved for implying contempt or sarcasm in a situation where a clearly expressed opinion could result in a severely bent nose. What the brain is doing with its audio transmitter (voice) and receiver (ear) is miraculous in its rendering but, none the less, quite obviously "learned".

All learning begins with the mental faculty of memory - another gift. The brain that cannot remember cannot learn because learning itself is essentially controlled memory. Words are repeated over and over until we remember their "sound-pattern" and what that particular sound symbolizes. The sound and the object begin to merge in the brain as a single thing. Language does not come "naturally"; it is a learned conditioned response to particular sound-patterns given "meaning" by other members of our linguistic group. It is invented and is THE most unnatural thing that humans do! Every time I say "finger", you'll get a visual flash from your memory banks of your finger. Not your mother's finger - your finger - because you have been conditioned to that response! The sound symbol "ball" conjures up a visual image of a sphere - not a cube - because "our" brain has been conditioned to relate the arbitrary, audible, English, symbol, "ball" to the physical shape of a sphere, (actually, because you're reading this, you are responding to "visual symbols". We'll get to read'n and rite'n soon, but first we should review the spoken language because it preceded writing by tens of thousands of years.)

Spoken language is a complex audio interaction of brain, ear, mouth parts, larynx and breathing apparatus. It requires the coordinated use of all three units - ear, brain, voice - working together before meaningful speech can be promoted. This is the hardware. The software, the program, is language itself - the carrier of information. The larynx generates the continuous sound wave and the mouth parts impress on that sound wave (modulates, if you like) the audio inflections learned by the ear as words; all controlled by the brain and mediated by the mind. Language is made up of "words" which are simply voice sounds, called phonemes, which have been assigned as "auditory symbols" to represent something - a tree, a rock, a house, etc. A modern English desk dictionary would have over 82,000 entrees to define the various words and phrases in current use. But this collection of words only defines those sound symbols still in current use. Many more sound symbols have faded from use or have been redefined, than are in use today. The English of only 400 years ago is very much a foreign language to the modern ear. Pure Shakespeare is unintelligible to the non-scholar because many words are no longer in use and the sentence structure (syntax) often sounds backward. The combination of odd words, accent and jumbled syntax conveys little meaning today. To understand Elizabethan English one must study the objects, conditions, writing, word definitions and pronunciations current to that time. And if you can appreciate how foreign past language sounds to us, you can understand how foreign our modern speech would sound to Medieval man. The only reason we can extract meaning from the "English" language prior to about 1400 AD is because of the work of scholars translating archaic words and phrases into modern English.

The English language is about half German and half French-Latin, with large chunks of Greek and bits of Arabic thrown in. It had its beginning about 700 AD but could only be recognized as "English" by a linguist. So if you ever get a chance to travel back in time, don't go any further than about 400 years, because you wouldn't be able to understand anyone. More to the point, no one would understand you, and your wonderful knowledge of the modern world could be a serious impediment to your health. They'd either burn you at the stake or put you in the loony-bin in 13th century England.

The growth of language was an excruciatingly slow process because, until phonetic writing, it had to be remembered from generation to generation. A language usually died with the civilization it gave birth to. The process, it could hardly be called the birth, of language may have begun about 1.5 million years ago because cranial studies indicate a slightly larger left hemisphere of the brain at that time. The left side of the brain of modern man is known to be associated with language and meaning and is larger than the right side.

About 500,000 years ago the rate of growth of the brain peaked at about 200 cubic centimeters every hundred thousand years. No other organ in the history of life has been found to have grown so fast. By 100,000 years ago, the brain had reached its present size of about 1345 cc. It should be kept in mind that this is a volume measurement. The surface area of the brain, where the higher centers of sensory and intellectual activities are located, is determined by the amount of folding of the outer neuron layer. This folding can greatly increase surface area without affecting the volume of the cranial cavity. Unfortunately, soft brain tissue is not preserved when animal remains are fossilized. Therefore we do not know if primitive brains were less convoluted. There is no clear evidence of increasing surface area with time; thus we can only equate intelligence with cranial capacity, and must conclude that intellectual capacity has remained unchanged for about 100,000 years. Neanderthal skulls, with capacities of 1600 cc have turned up! So we Homo Sapiens, who shared Europe with the Neanderthals about 50,000 years ago, are still scratching our primate skulls about whether we were smarter or just more vicious than these gentle giants. We are fond of depicting the Neanderthal as a hulking, beetle-browed brute, but he may have begun the process of the ritual burial of his dead. Neanderthal graves have included food, charcoal, weapons and the body bedecked with flowers. Mute testimony to a sensitivity at least equal to our own to-day. The Neanderthals died out 40,000 years ago; about 10,000 years after our ancestors came onto the playing field.

Until visual symbols (writing) were invented about 5500 years ago, language was very tenuous. Because audible symbols could exist only so long as memory could hold them, whole languages containing thousands of years of understanding could be wiped out in a single generation by war, pestilence or drought.

English is one of the languages, of a family of tongues, called Indo-European. It traces backward in cultural history through Low German, West German, and Germanic to Indo-European. The "Indo" part is from Sanskrit, an early language traced to Northern India. Ancient Greek, Italic (Latin), Germanic and Celtic are the four basic tongues of the "European" part. These Indo-European dialects are spoken by almost two-thirds of humanity.

Latin (100 BC) was the language of the Roman Empire and was the official speech of the government, church and education of England, at one time. With the fall of the Western Roman Empire around 500 AD, the invading Germanic tribes brought new words and ideas into the lexicon of Medieval Latin writings. By 800 AD Classical Latin was dead; no longer understood or spoken by the people, but living on in the Roman Catholic Church and in legal documents. Classical Latin is a very sophisticated tongue capable of expressing the most subtle aspects of Philosophy or Law; most of the versatility of English, as a language, is due to its Latin content. Science and technology would be almost speechless without this "dead" language. Classical Latin slowly evolved into the Romans (Romance) tongues of French, Spanish, Portuguese, Romanian, and of course Italian.

As a method of preserving knowledge, written language (visual symbols) is only slightly less fragile than the spoken word! If the visual symbols are not passed on by memorized-learning, their "meaning" can disappear almost as quickly as the spoken symbols. Egyptian Hieroglyphics, a form of picture writing, began about 3100 BC and slowly evolved into more abstract symbols as the centuries rolled by. The Egyptian civilization finally collapsed about 700 BC. After more than 3000 years of progress, it took whole armies to carry off the accumulated riches; Persians (525 BC), Greeks (332 BC), Romans (30 BC), Arabs (641), Turks (1517), French (1798), Arabs (1805) and British (1882) all over-ran the Pearl of the Nile and picked at her carcass. The written language of Egypt was still in use around 200 BC because it was then that a priestly decree, in three separate scripts (hieroglyphics, demotic and Greek), was struck into a slab of black basalt: at the town of Rosetta, Egypt. The Romans, who arrived in 30 BC, couldn't find anyone who could read the hieroglyphics and they were unaware of the stone at Rosetta, now broken and buried by sand. Somewhere between 200 BC and 30 BC the last faint echo of spoken Egyptian slipped beneath the whispering sand. Today, we can "read" the ancient Egyptian writing because in 1799 the French army discovered a broken piece (about 3 ft. long) of the Rosetta Stone that provided the base for deciphering the hieroglyphics. The piece of stone was invaluable because its message was repeated in three separate scripts. The middle script, demotic, was a simplified cursive form of the 1st script, hieroglyphic, while the 3rd script was in known Greek. From about 200 BC to 1800 AD, the Egyptian language had not been spoken, read or written for 2000 years! The hieroglyphic visual symbols that remain are not phonetic. We shall never know what the Egyptian language "sounded" like because its voice died when the civilization it created died. Today the oral and written language of Egypt is Arabic, not Egyptian.

The Sumerians, between the Tigris and Euphrates rivers in modern Iraq, developed pictograms about 3500 BC. The Egyptians developed hieroglyphics about 3100 BC while the Chinese were creating a stylized pictorial script. The Phoenicians, today's coastal Israel and Lebanon, from their city of Byblos (near Beirut) introduced a type of "phonetic" writing to the Greeks about 1500 BC. This phonetic writing differed from picture writing in that a completely abstract squiggle or mark was used to indicate (symbolize) a particular "sound" that the voice could make. But it wasn't pure - it had no symbols to represent the vowel sounds (a e i o u y) but had other symbols that represented combined sounds or syllables. This lack of vowel sounds was also a feature of the Semitic Alphabet, used to record the early Hebrew writings that were to become the Bible. The absence of vowel sound symbols makes interpretation of these early phonetic writings somewhat ambiguous.

The Greeks replaced some of the Phoenician syllable letters with vowel signs and created the first true alphabet of vowels and consonants only. Papyrus from Egypt reached Greece via the city of Byblos; and its form, rolled into a cylinder or scroll, became "biblion", the Greek word for rolled paper. The words "Bible" and "bibliography" originate from the same city-source. The Greek words for the first two letters of their "word generator" are "alpha" and "beta". When joined together, these two Greek letters give us the English word "alphabet", which represents our own 26 letter word generator; the first two letters of which are A and B.

The alphabet we have today came to us through the Romans, who gave the 20 letters inherited from the Greeks, Latin sounds and added 3 of their own (k, y and z) for a 23 letter Latin alphabet. English speaking peoples added the letter symbols of the sounds J, V, and W to give the 26 letter phonetic alphabet that makes up the 83 thousand +, words (and still growing) of their language.

Speaking a language is a complex interaction of voice-brain-ear; but it is learned.

Reading a language is a complex interaction of eye-brain; but it is learned.

Writing a language is a complex interaction of eye-brain-hand; but it is learned.

Language is a learned conditioned response in all its various modes of expression through audible, visual or tactile coded symbols. It has its roots in the gift of speech and has its greatest expression in the brain of man. Reading and writing are important adjuncts to the tongues of man but the foundation of language is the spoken word. And the words are physical audible symbols generated by the brain-mouth; carried by a physical medium (air); and received by a separate brain-ear. They begin as patterns that the brain slowly learns to recognize as having some kind of "meaning" because they are repeated over and over again. The patterns of neuron stimulation come from an area of the brain that interprets this stimulus as "sound", so these are sound patterns. They are different from the other brain locations that interpret their stimuli as light, pressure, taste or smell etc.

Even though each separate area gets its information in the same format (nerve signals), the interpretation is different.

The mind may lie here, in the diffused neural inter-connections between the sensory areas; we don't know. It is probably the mind that allows the brain to associate correspondence (water is wet, heavy, tasteless, fluid etc.) between the senses; but again, we don't know.

We do know that a sound pattern (word) can be used to represent (name) something; that the audible symbol "eye" can be the word identifier for the organ of sight; that the word "father" can be used to represent a male parent - yet only in English does that "sound" have that meaning. In another language, a different sound symbol is used to express that same "meaning". In German it's "fader"; Spanish, "padre"; Latin, "pater" and in Sanskrit it's "pitar". These are all related or "cognate" words of different languages and literally means "words born together". They represent the changes that have taken place as the Indo-European family of tongues evolved in both time and place. Language is changing and growing continuously to accommodate a group's changing life-styles. More words in any language leads to greater utility of that language. These five separate linguistic groups can each express the concept or meaning of a male parent, but none can understand the other. Each can "think" with great clarity, in their own language, but cannot express the simplest idea to the other groups.

Language is not only used for talking to our neighbor but, more importantly, for talking to our "selves". We need language to think. In all the articles I've read, regarding language, ALL recognize the utility of language in "thinking". All admit it is "hard to think without it" or "difficult to express ideas or complex concepts without it", or "almost impossible to express abstract ideas without it". ALL refuse to take the final step and say, "Hey man, I CAN'T THINK without it". It's easy enough to say! The sky hasn't fallen! Why all the trepidation? Because of what that statement means. It means the Emperor has no clothes! That final step brings us to the very edge of a mental black hole that is truly terrifying. Very few people have ever looked directly into its yawning maw and none can look for long. For it is here that the inner self teeters, literally, on the brink of reality and abstraction!

If we admit that we invented language and that we can't think without it, then we have, in effect, invented ourselves. We don't exist! "We" are a kind of dream located somewhere between the real neurons of our physical brain. If language is invented and we ourselves assigned the definitions of its sound symbols (words), how can anything have any "real" meaning? Language, the conveyer of meaning, is a string of sound symbols, arbitrarily assigned a meaning by our own minds. Our minds are where we think;

where "we" exist. But we can only think with words, and words are what language is; and if language is meaningless, then thinking is too. One can get a headache or go nuts just thinking about it, let alone talking about it. Do you begin to see the problem? Do you see what language is?

Saying what you "mean" and "meaning" what you say, is the audible equivalent of the visual illusion of the "vase or two heads": both flip back and forth in our audible or visual memory as to interpretation. One moment we hear or see one interpretation, and the next moment, we hear or see the other "meaning". It is difficult to understand that the same "thing" can be interpreted differently and yet has not physically changed! Don't waste your time trying to unravel these two conundrums - they are only to illustrate that each of us may (NOT can or will) have a different interpretation of exactly the same "reality", even though "reality" itself never changes. It is the patterns in the brains stationary neurons that are shifting. A words "meaning" is determined by its position within the structure of words that make up the sentence (pattern) as a whole. Understanding is not achieved overnight. It takes weeks, months and years for the existing patterns of meaning, as expressed by words and groups of words already in the brains associative memory, to be arranged into a new lattice-work of interconnections. It is enough if you appreciate that the addition of a single word, to already existing vocabulary, can drastically shift the overall pattern into a new perception of reality. Reality, truth, never changes, only how we perceive it. And language, words, sound-patterns, are the "eyes" of the brain's mind; the 5th dimension. Language gives meaning to everything; literally.

Everyone agrees that language is invented. The tricky part is, can we think without it! We can all "remember" any information that our sensors bring in, but that is called day dreaming. One doesn't need words to remember what ones room "looks" like or how nice the music "sounded" last week; or does one? In order to remember any "particular" event or stimuli, you need a word identifier in order to select it. But as soon as you use a "word" identifier, we're back to language and thinking again

Given that day-dreaming is remembering without the use of language, let's take the final step to the edge of infinity and say, "Without language, I cannot think". Because you are the "source", I cannot tell "you" what to think, but as for "myself", "I" have just become an abstraction. Existing, if that is the word for it, only in my mind, which is a creation of language that was invented by itself! "I" have all the substance of the "grin" that was left behind when the Cheshire cat vanished in "Alice in Wonderland". My sense of inner-self is a side effect of my bodies acquired linguistic code: or as Rene Descartes has said, "I think, therefore I am".

My body hasn't vanished. My brain and the universe are still here. But when I accepted that last premise of "thinking is an expression of language" (rather than the other way around), the Cosmos shimmered ever so slightly in the mind's visual field. The universe has changed forever. A new dimension has been added to the universe, and its units of measure are words; abstract audible symbols assigned arbitrary meaning; language; mind-speak. The total assembly of words and the facility with which they are used defines the limits of this new dimension. It is different for each brain. We shall call it the 5th dimension and it may be just another expression for the word "mind" or the word "language".

The rational for naming it the 5th dimension is because the other four are already spoken for. The first three are the dimensions of physical space and are measured in the units of length, width and depth. The 4th dimension of space is measured in seconds, and is called time. All matter and energy in the universe is understood to exist in a 4 dimensional space-time continuum; the length, width and depth of space, which then persists in time.

The 5th dimension of mind is measured in vocabulary and adroit use of language (intelligence) and may be generated in the brain of living humans. It is the location of everything that is abstract to the human brain, and that is a very great deal indeed - including the sense of self.

But hey, let's not get our shorts in knot as to the philosophical question of personal existence! We can discuss it later, after we learn a bit more about language and the nature of things. After all, that haunting cry of "Who am I?" has echoed down the halls of history in a million different tongues, for fifty thousand years. You can wait a bit yet. The only reason I mentioned it in this section is to help drive home the "understanding" of what language is to mankind. It is everything!

Many "reasons" for mans supremacy and uniqueness on earth have been given. He discovered the use of fire; he invented the wheel; he uses tools; walks on two legs; has an opposable thumb; he is naked, without fur; he clothes himself; builds his own residence; builds bridges; builds dams; has a big brain, and on and on. Some have merit, others just a silly expressions of self-love, narcissism. But for some strange reason, none seems to have picked-up on his greatest invention, language; the one thing that has telescoped the natural evolutionary process of environmental adaptation from fifty thousand years to a single generation; your generation. The one thing that allowed him to put another log on the fire; put an axle to the wheel, put a handle on the hammer-head; put shoes on his feet and gloves on his hands; put a zipper on his fly and a new blade in the razor; put doors and windows on his house; build the bridge where the road-way was located and put the dam where the water-way was narrowest and strongest; the thing that is the base of his intelligence, language. The one thing that allowed him to think and to be whatever he is inclined to be; a doctor, lawyer, philosopher, farmer, or any of the millions of various occupations and endeavors that he lays his mind to; language.

The only superlative that comes close to, but does not equal the brilliance of, that guttural sound "language" is the word "man". The societies of man could not exist without the invention of language. The institutions of government, religion, law and medicine would not exist without the words to express them!

To man the individual and mankind the group, language is everything.

Why is it that the brain uses words (sound symbols) with which to think - what's so special about sound? Perhaps, when the Pharyngeal Pouch, with its tiny Ossicles, migrated to the middle ear, it took some nerves with it. That could mean that a small group of brain neurons in the speech control center are being stimulated from both larynx and middle ear. No larger than a grain of rice but containing thousands of cells! That nerve link could represent the reflex-arc that promotes the conditioned response that resulted in "language", which allows the brain to establish associative aural patterns with the patterns of other areas of perception, that we call abstract thinking. After all, we do think with sound patterns (words)!

We use words, and not pictures, to think. We are not, like fireflies, equipped with a light-generating system for signaling - which is great if your nocturnal, but we aren't. If we had a TV tube stuck in our forehead, that gave a visual display of brain activity then maybe language would have evolved into pictures; but we don't and it didn't. Many animals, including our selves, have elaborate "body language" signals; but these don't work well at night or in fog or thick bush - they have to be seen to be useful. Sound does indeed seem to be a very good medium for the transmission of information in our external environment. It is interesting that sound wave transmission in air is a close parallel to the ionic wave transmission in a nerve fiber. The air-wave is a series of compressions and rarefactions that can vary only in frequency and intensity. Both these physical phenomena are transmitted, by the mechanical action of the middle ear and the fluid of the inner ear, to the sensory cells in the cochlea. The different locations of cells respond to different frequencies and each has its own nerve, to carry the ionic wave produced, into its own brain cell. The velocity of the air sound wave is about 1/3 faster (340 to 200 msec.) than the nerve ionic wave. The ionic wave is identified by a succession of electrical peaks traveling up the nerve fiber; the sound wave is identified by a succession of pressure peaks traveling through the air. For sound wave transmission one doesn't have to see the transmitter in order to receive its signal; it works day or night, seen or unseen. And the really neat thing about it is that once you've learned an audible code, it can be used internally - to talk with your "self" - to think. And it gives your brain, access to the brain of anything else that has learned your audible code. The separate minds of men are tied together and influenced collectively by language.

In addition to conveying abstract ideas by groups of words, single words are used as behavioral modifiers - much more than you were aware. "Yes" and "No" are the first behavioral modifiers used to control your activities. For too many parents, the "No" is often followed by a physical slap. The slap produces pain and causes the body's natural defense-reflex to avoid the blow. The child "winces". Because the slap hurts, the child cries. In ALL cases of physical abuse, when the child hears the word "NO", it will stop whatever it is doing, "wince" and begin to cry - even if the slap is not delivered! The abusive parent has treated his child to a trained (but cruelly inappropriate), conditioned response to the word "NO", just as Pavlov's dogs salivated to the "sound" of a bell. When you say "NO" to your child, does he "wince"?

Just as words can and do initiate trained conditioned response in the physical body, they initiate trained conditioned response in the neurons of the brain. We can train our bodies to do particular things with considerable precision, just by repeating an action over and over; such as walking or running or hand-stands or gymnastics. Just so, "we" (the mind) can train the brain to remember particular sound patterns with considerable precision, just by repeating the word (sound pattern) over and over; such as memorizing the assigned meaning of words or putting the words together to make a sentence or making the sentences into stories or making stories express ideas that have never been expressed before. Like we are doing now!

This is the power of language - it can cause the flesh to move and the brain to think.

Language is the ONLY means into or out of the mind. Language is the two-way link between the 5th dimension and reality; between what is abstract and what is real. Language is used to define what is abstract and what is real. Language gives meaning to the word "meaning". Meaning IS language.

Because the 5th dimension is measured by vocabulary and its use and words, the units of language, are stored in real brain cells - it is the "meaning" of language that is abstract, and is how the mind came into being. The "mind" is the "meaning" in language. That is how mind "exists" between the neurons of the brain. The neurons are stationary, but they hold patterns of words as ionic suspensions that can "read-in" or "read-out" meaning. The 5th dimension has been with man ever since he first assigned an audible sound to symbolize a physical object. The 5th dimension started forming with that first word, and has been growing ever since. Every time a new word is added, the utility of the total sum of words preceding it doubles. If you have 500 words to delineate the size of your particular 5th dimension (we each get only one, fortunately) and you add one word, the value of the other 500 doubles to a thousand! This isn't true - it is just a convenient strategy that is almost true, to demonstrate how each new word may increase the usefulness of one's vocabulary as a whole. For example the sound symbol "evolution", and what it means, had an enormous effect on the mind of man. One sound symbol changed the world as man viewed it; through the lattice work patterns of words and meaning, created by his language. Languages that man him-self invented - and he didn't even know what he was doing.

So please, my friend, do not be afraid of new sound patterns such as the "5th dimension"; or the "5th state of matter" - the living cells that gave it birth. New ideas require minor realignment of words and meaning, in order that they can be expressed. Don't worry; be happy - for something new and wonderful may begin to happen, inside your head, as you come to understand that language is the creator of worlds. Language is to your human cultural "self" what genes are to your human biological body.

It is classic irony that wisdom may have come to know itself just moments before it died! Language has its home in mankind, and humanity is threatening its own existence and the continuance of all other life-forms on this planet. This precious orb may very well be the only home of all life in the entire universe; we know of none other than this.

Language, how do I love thee? You are understanding!

"Man is the measure of all things" Protagoras (485-410 B.C.) Athens, Greece.

"Man is the namer of all things" James H. Washer, 2008 A.D., Athens, Ontario, Canada.

A Tale of the Snake

Ever wonder why a snake wiggles when it walks?

It is such an odd way to get around that I tried many times to find the answer. There were several explanations to be found, but each answer pleased for only a little while and then became unsatisfactory again. One of the first that seemed to make sense was the comparison of a man trying to carry a twenty-foot piece of pipe through a dense forest. To a small snake, the high grass seemed like a dense forest. The only way he could get through it was to bend his body to avoid the stubble. Made sense! So I could forget about the snake for awhile. But then I'd see the snake on clear ground, and he still wiggled when he walked. I reasoned that since each part of the snake had to take a zigzag path, its net forward movement would always be less than the actual path traveled - that is, in order for the snake to progress one mile, his body would have to walk about two miles!

It seemed a terrible waste of energy and shoe-leather. Also, dew-worms didn't wiggle when they walked! So back to the library. I found out that a snake has ribs and that when it moved; it was actually walking on its ribs. It also has hips! Under the skin, about three-quarters of the way back from the head, was a set of vestigial legs, co-incident with the shrunken hips. These shrunken remains of hips and legs showed that at one time, long ago, the snake had real legs to walk about with. A comparison was then made to modern lizards and how, because of side-mounted short legs, they threw their bodies into "S" shaped curves in order to get maximum use of legs too short. The snake had simply kept this body movement after its legs were gone!

Well, there it was - the answer. A little more involved than carrying a pipe through thick forest, but it did make sense. I was undisturbed for a few more years.

But a snake can crawl quite nicely through a straight piece of pipe and it has no trouble crawling into relatively straight mouse tunnels, to get its prey! That is, if it has to, it can travel in a straight line; if it doesn't have to travel in a straight line, it wiggles, or more to the point, the "S" shape is not required for moving the ribs on which the snake walks. Back to the books. Unfortunately, I couldn't find the right book; none that I poured through gave an answer that seemed reasonable.

I was twenty-six (approx.) before finding the answer. The problem had been nagging at me for weeks and I was thoroughly sick of it. There was a young lad working in my department who was particularly clever, and he was fresh out of school. I decided to bounce the question off him, cold turkey. His answer nearly took my head off. It was like a thousand flashbulbs went off in my brain - I was stunned (again). I mumbled "what?" and he elaborated slightly; but it wasn't necessary - I knew.

My somewhat over-reaction was due to the answer's simple brilliance, and my incredible stupidity at not coming up with the answer myself. There was no need to have read a single snake book (but I'm glad I did.); the answer is that simple and that obvious. I'll tell you what he said in a minute, but can you guess?

This is a good example of the difference between knowing and understanding. I knew more about the locomotion of a snake than I knew about my own locomotion, but still didn't understand why it wiggled when it walked. I understood why man waves his arms while walking - it aids in balance. I was loaded with information about the snake, but didn't understand. Knowing things comes about by simply collecting and storing bits of information, and then juggling those bits about to make different chunks of knowledge.

Understanding comes from recognizing the obvious. Understanding is seeing the simple logic of relationships. It is a difficult concept to get across because language itself is interpreted slightly different by each of us; which is why I've used this little story to get the idea across. We have all experienced those moments when we've asked ourselves. "Why the hell didn't I think of that?" They are usually preceded by an event called understanding, which feels like revelation, and succeeded, by the comment, "I knew that!"

Oh! The answer I got was, "So it doesn't roll over"! Stability, balance. The serpentine form of body position allows the snake to cross a hill without rolling like a piece of pipe into the valley.

I never had the courage to ask him how he knew. Shortly after that, I noticed that a Camel has an odd way of walking. Did you ever wonder why a Camel swings both legs, on the same side of his body, at the same time! Well, the reason that is so different from the way practically all other quadrupeds walk is because of the.... but that's another story; we want to know about you, not Camels.

To understand who and what "you" are, why and when you do the things you do, requires going back to a time before you came into existence

Understanding doesn't come easy - you have to work very hard at accumulating the bits of truth (factual knowledge) that makes up reality. You will find many truths hard to accept because they appear to lead to conclusions that demean the generally accepted status of man-the-magnificent. You will find that we actually know very little about what reality is - our minds are stuffed with things that are nonsense, which actually impede understanding, until we can recognize them as irrelevant.

Understanding doesn't come cheap - there is an emotional price to pay that many will be unwilling or unable, to make. It places a severe drain on the intellectual currency of anyone. It may cost you your very soul. Understanding is when discord blends into harmony or chaos changes into order - the transition point is not always obvious. Insight into why an animal does anything comes from knowledge of how the animal relates to its environment. The animal and its environment are inextricably linked; they are one. We must have knowledge of both to understand either. They are one harmonious whole.

The journey doesn't end with this little book; it is only a guide to help you on your way. If there is a purpose or a destination to our journey, I don't know what it is. But perhaps you will provide the answer to that; after all, you are the source whether you like it or not. Think before you proceed.

Chapter 4

The External Environment:

The universe is unfolding as it should.

Welcome to the 5th dimension. Hope your peek into the mental black hole wasn't too scary. Please consider me as your guide from now on; as the source, you are your own teacher/pupil and will naturally "see" things differently from me because you each have your own 5th dimension, or mind.

The 5th dimension is constructed of words. Because words have real existence as physical vibrations in the air or as letters typed on a piece of paper, there is a certain aspect of "reality" to the 5th dimension as well. Although the brain uses words with which to think, it feels more comfortable with a "vision" to relate to; so I will suggest a few "structures" to use as visual analogs of the 5th dimension. Note: this peculiar need of the brain to have a graphic base for its abstract musing is also responsible for much misunderstanding about the universe or man, as being machines. *A picture is worth a thousand words.*

We could think of the 5th dimension as a box that is constructed of "words", and the meanings of the words could then be contained in the box. We could form some of the words into "boards" and then use other words to "nail" the word-boards into the shape of a box. The more words or vocabulary you had, the more word-boards you could make and the bigger would be your 5th dimensional box of meanings. That is all learning is.

Or we could think of each word as separate pieces of a large puzzle. Each word could be fitted with other words until their individual meanings formed a word-picture of something. The words could be re-arranged to vary their separate meanings, just like real sentences do, and you could thus make all kinds of different word-pictures simply by re-arranging the same word pieces. The more word pieces you had, the more pictures you could make and the bigger would be your 5th dimension. That is all a book is.

Another way of looking at it, and the one I shall use, is to compare the 5th dimension of language to a large (not too large, - let not pride displace modesty) lattice-work sphere. The words make-up the lattice-work, and inside the sphere of words, are their meanings. By looking through the lattice-work of words, I can see the meanings of those words swirling around inside. The advantage of this word-lattice is that it can change its patterns from moment to moment. They can be diamond shaped or square shaped or crystal shaped or rectangular or whatever. But each change or mix of patterns gives me a different view of the "meanings" inside. The more words I add to the lattice-work sphere, the larger will be my 5th dimension of meaning and understanding. That is what the mind is.

Inside the lattice-word sphere, in addition to the "meaning" of words and sentences, will be other abstract things. Things that you do not think of as abstract; not existing in reality. We will be tossing all these "things" into the 5th dimension, as we go along. One of the first things to go in, are the meanings of words. Words are quite meaningless to something not trained in the use of their arbitrary assignment to represent "something"; their meaning is abstract, exists only in the mind.

"Meaning" is assigned - it is arbitrary - it is abstract - it does not exist. That is why we've constructed our 5th dimension; to give the "meaning" of words a place to "be"; a home. Still confused? Relax and keep your sense of humor handy. You will come to your own appreciation (or rejection) of the 5th dimension in your own good time.

The arrival of life introduced some qualities to the universe that had never existed before. Just as each material state of matter has the general qualities of gas, liquid or solid; and these three states have characteristics peculiar to themselves that have no expression in the others (a "gas" can't be crystalline, a "solid" can't flow, a "liquid" cannot be hard, in their natural states), so it is with living matter. (Absorbs nutrients from its environment and reproduces itself).

To understand the "Source", we must know a bit of what the universe was like before "life" came into existence. And I must emphasize a "bit" here. Our natural sensors are detecting far less than 1% of what is actually out there in our external environment. We know practically nothing yet; and everything that we do know has come in as a coded signal on the nerve fibers of our internal environment. The coded signals are often misread. This book is another reading of those signals and may itself be a misinterpretation. That is why you, the source, buried at the end of your own nerve fiber network, must make the interpretation! You are the only one who can; you must know more.

No one knows how it all began. The present favorite is the "Big Bang" theory, but it is only the latest guess. Hopefully, you will have at least some knowledge of stars, galaxies, supernova, planets, gravity, etc. and the immensity of the space occupied by our 15 billion year old, expanding universe. We will begin with the planet Earth about 3 billion years ago - just before life made its appearance. But first, a few comments on basics.

SPACE; Nothing; a place between bits of matter but devoid of matter itself.

We think energy (force) and time may exist in space, independent of matter. It may be that space is only a convenience concept required by the brain that says something cannot exist in nothing. If matter exists, it must exist "in" something. In any case, it represents a very serious problem for physics - action at a distance - and is the principle culprit responsible for the recently emerged theories of Quantum Mechanics. Action at a distance has haunted man ever since he first noticed that separate chunks of matter will sometime affect each other without touching. How does a magnet attract a piece of iron; what is an electric field?

A problem in the late 1800's was that electromagnetic energy, such as light and heat radiation, were understood to have a wave form. Now in order for a wave to exist, there had to be a medium to support the wave; otherwise, how do we get light and heat from the Sun! You can have water without waves but you cannot have water-waves without the water. So it was understood that a substance called aether pervaded all space between matter. The aether could be the substance that waved and supported the electric and magnetic fields. Then the ingenious experiments of Michelson and Morely proved aether didn't exist! Newton's original light-corpuscles were resurrected until quantum mechanics could establish the photon as the carrier of electromagnetic energy. Quantum Mechanics now specifies an intermediate vector particle, which is exchanged through space, for all action at distance phenomena. Space is given the dimensions of length, width and depth so that matter might exist in it. In the early 1900's, as a result of Einstein's' theories of relativity, "time" was added to the three spatial dimensions to provide for the 4 dimensions of the "space / time continuum" required for the persistence of all matter.

MATTER: Anything that has mass and occupies space and time.

All matter is made up of atoms, of which there are about 92 stable types, which make up the basic natural elements. Each element has its own characteristic mass. These 92 elements combine physically to make up all the various material forms in the universe. The air, earth, water, fire, plants, animals, stars, galaxies, the human body, the brain; are all made up of matter. The atom is mostly empty space. Its nucleus is about one trillionth the size of the volume traced by its speeding electrons.

The electrons of different elements interact in determined ways to form the various compounds. Ninety-nine percent of everything around "you" is a compound of two or more elements. We rarely experience the pure elements in their natural form. Protons and neutrons make up the atom nucleus and are, in turn, believed to be made up of smaller particles called quarks. These natural elements are stable because the negative charges on the electrons are normally perfectly balanced by the positive charge of the protons; the neutrons carry no charge. A whole zoo of additional particles, says quantum mechanics, flicker between the basic quark, proton, neutron, electron components, to keep everything from blowing apart or imploding due to the dynamic, electric and magnetic stress of its parts.

This is not to suggest the natural atoms are unstable! Far from it; they are the model of stability. The atoms are the proverbial Rock of Ages; it takes a mighty hammer-blow to break the atom, and as much energy to put one together. There is nothing at all wrong with the atom, but we have great difficulty understanding how or why its stays together.

The problem is that as we see it, all the positive charges are in the nucleus. Like charges repel - so why doesn't the nucleus blow itself apart? All the negative charges are whirling around the nucleus - why don't they fly apart because of like charge, or, because of unlike-charge, rush into the nucleus to join up with the positive proton? That's the puzzle quantum mechanics is trying to explain. There is much we do not understand about matter. Strong and weak nuclear forces are now proposed to account for atomic stability.

The atom of hydrogen is the simplest, stable, natural element of all matter. So far, it appears that 99% of the material of stars and galaxies consist of hydrogen atoms. It is believed that most of the other elemental atoms were made from hydrogen gas in the crucible of the Super-Nova. The lighter first four or five elements can form and stabilize in the average life-cycle of a star, but it takes the energy and relatively short duration of a Super Nova to create, and then leave behind, the heavier elements.

The problem is that one; the atoms require enormous energy to crush the protons close-enough together that they will "stick" despite the repulsive force of their positive charge, and two; that enormous energy must be immediately withdrawn, or it will knock asunder that which it just "stuck" together. It is believed that much of the matter you see about you, including the heavy elements of the compounds that make up your body and brain, most came into being in the short, intense, pulse of energy produced by Super-Nova long past. You are made from the stuff of stars.

The vast majority of "stars" are now known to be binary or clusters of stars. Our Sun is a very rare "singlet" star. Perhaps our Sun once had a companion that was destroyed by a near-by Super-Nova (relatively speaking) a long, long time ago, and part of the debris accrued into the present Solar system.

Mass is a characteristic of matter measured in terms of inertia. On the earth's surface, the acceleration of mass caused by gravity, is called "weight". This "weight" is in fact an "effect" of the earth's gravitational field on that mysterious quality of matter called inertia. The inertia is an almost invariant quality of matter; as stable as the atoms themselves. Inertia is the resistance to motion, or once moving, the resistance to being stopped. All matter in motion moves in a straight line unless acted on by an outside force. Inertia is mysterious because one has not the slightest inkling that it is there until one tries to accelerate a piece of matter.

GRAVITY; The ancient ones never imagined a "force" held things clinging to the earth's flat surface. Material things such as rocks or water "fell" and immaterial things, such as fire or vapors "rose", because that is what they "wanted" to do. It was normal; any fool could see that that was so. Heavy things fell faster because their "want" was greater. Four "elements" made up the material universe, earth, water, air and fire.

Galileo proved, in the 1590's, that heavy and light objects all fell at the same rate, and Newton, in the 1670's, decided there was some kind of attraction that caused material particles to attract each other with a "force" that was proportional to the product of their masses and inversely proportional to the square of the distance between their centers. He called the force "gravity" and went on to demonstrate that gravity held the moon in its orbit about the earth.

Today, international agreement places the sea level gravitational acceleration at about 980.6 cm/sec sq. At the poles it exceeds, 983 and at the equator is about 978 cm/sec sq. That means you weigh a bit more at the poles than you would at the equator. On the equator, because the earth is an oblate spheroid, you are about 14 mi. further from the earth's centre than at the poles; even though you have 14 more miles of "attractive" rock between you and the centre, you weigh less (than at the poles) because you are further away.

Einstein, who gave us the famous mass = energy formula of $E = mc^2$, (mass x speed of light squared), had some misgivings about gravity and finally suggested that maybe gravity was an "effect" and not a force at all! He had an Equivalence Principle, that any experiment done in a gravitational field would have precisely the same results if conducted in a room having a motion-acceleration rate equal to the gravity acceleration; i.e. actual acceleration of matter, caused the equivalent effects of matter at rest in a gravity field. He suspected gravity may be an effect of the "warping" of 4 dimensional space / time by a piece of matter. That a large piece of matter (a planet), as a concentration of energy, warps the surrounding space/time it is in, such that a smaller piece of matter (a meteorite) in that space is simply rolling down a space/time slope. What we see is the "effect" of an invisible slope, not a gravity "force" attracting the object.

ENERGY and FORCE: Energy is defined as the capacity or ability to perform work. Force is defined as a push or a pull. But there is much misunderstanding about which is what! Some believe that energy floods the entire universe as a kind of "flux" and that matter is points of energy-condensation in the space/time continuum. It comes in an almost endless variety of roles - mechanical energy, potential energy, kinetic energy, solar energy, chemical energy, gravitational energy, electrical energy, nuclear energy, atomic energy, and on and on. Many "forces" are now known to be the effects of the normal operation of natural laws, but because they were named before we discovered they did not exist as forces, we are stuck with anachronisms that detract, rather than add, to understanding.

Centrifugal or "center fleeing" force is the "pull" we experience when going around a curve in a speeding vehicle or when we whirl a rock on a string. Although the "force" seems to pull straight outward from the center of rotation, it disappears the instant the restraining (centripetal) force is removed. Actually, the force is the "effect" of the resistance that a moving inertial body offers to deflection from a straight line; it is an inertial effect to constrained motion.

Science presently recognizes only four forces in nature; gravity, electromagnetic, strong and the weak nuclear forces.

Gravity: mediates the interaction of large masses, such as the planets, stars and galaxies. It is the weakest of all the forces; and its range is infinite.

Electromagnetic; mediates the interaction of small masses, such as the valance bonds between atoms and molecules that gives the great variety of compounds we enjoy. It also allows the flow of radiant energy, via the photon, between our father, the Sun and our mother, the Earth. We use this force to power our homes and industries.

Weak nuclear force mediates the interaction of atomic structure; electron, proton, neutron and about 30 other particles. The weak force is hundreds of times weaker than the next force;

Strong nuclear force: holds the quarks together so protons and neutrons can persist.

In many ways, the concepts of "energy" and "force" are often seen to be no more than "convenience concepts" to help bridge the gap between a detected change and the cause or "reason" for that change. You might find things easier to understand if, every time you see the words "energy" or "force", you substitute the word affect or causal.

Energy and force are to science what deities and spirits are to religion. They are the mysterious "power" that, moves the universe and man.

TIME: The fourth dimension of a physical object; and with about equal substance to space. But time has become the "word tag" that we have attached to the phenomenon that allows a piece of matter to "persist", moment to moment, in the time slot we call "now"; the present. Like length, width and depth, "persistence in time" has become recognized (in the early 1900's) as a fundamental dimension for the existence of an object. It is something we have a sense of, but are not sure what that sensor is or where it's located. Human methods of marking time-intervals have been many. The apparent passage of the Sun gives a day and a night; the phases of the moon mark the month. In daylight, the progress of a shadow across the ground; sand or water running into or out of a vessel; at night, a glowing ember on a length of fiber, or a lighted candle slowly consuming itself; or noting the passage of stars in the sky. With the coming of gears, clock-works were invented that had methods of marking the hour, and eventually, minutes and seconds of the day.

As our understanding of the solar system ripened into maturity, these clock-work devises came to be understood as "analogs" of the earth's rotation on its axis. Each full earth rotation was divided into one 24 hr. day. Each hour was divided into 60 minutes and each minute into 60 seconds. Most clock-faces are marked off for 12 hours, which means the hour hand must make two complete rotations about the face in order to express one rotation of the earth. It is turning at twice the speed of the earth; so that means the earth's rotation is r-e-a-1-l-y slow. If you were on the equator, you'd be traveling at only 1,000 miles per hour; at the 45th parallel of latitude, about 500 miles per hour, and at the north or south pole, the hour hand would go around twice while you only went around once! Today, time is measured with atomic clocks and digital wrist-watches. Time, as measured in the life-span of man doesn't have much significance in a 15 billion year old universe. In fact, before life, time as we humans understand it may not have existed.

So there we have it! Space, matter, mass, force or energy, and time. The "stuff" of the universe, and all shrouded in mystery. The meanings of all these word-identifiers go into the lattice-word sphere of the 5th dimension. Only matter and mass itself are "real" and thus can remain outside. Space, force or energy and time do not appear to have physical reality; they are abstract concepts and must go inside the 5th dimension. I emphasize that this little review is but a sampling of the vast sum of knowledge available.

Whole libraries are filled with books on any one of these subjects. I focus on the unusual aspects of them to help demonstrate how fragile our understanding of nature is, and because it would be boring for you and tedious for me, to simply repeat what you already know. Your understanding of "self" will be directly related to how big your vocabulary of word-meaning is. Do not confuse the English word "matter" with the thing itself. In another language, the thing itself would be represented by another sound-pattern. Like-wise, do not confuse today's understanding of a word-tag with the ancients' understanding of the same word-tag. The "atom" of Democritus (500 BC) was a different "understanding" than the John Dalton atom of 1808; just as Dalton's atom is different from the Quantum atom of to-day. A words meaning is assigned by man and is quite variable. As near as we can determine, the Hydrogen atom hasn't changed a quark for the past 15 billion years. It is our "understanding" that is changing as our knowledge - base grows; you must know more. In the Middle Ages something called Phlogiston was believed to be a substance in all combustible bodies – the flame of fire.

For most of our history space has been the 3 dimensional container of all matter. In order for matter to persist it has to "continue" to occupy that space volume. If it did not exist in time, as well as in space, it would be gone after a moment had passed. This does not mean that all objects are moving at the speed of light - there is no motion being implied. It's just that we have this sense of time passing from past through the present and on into the future; or perhaps the other way around, from the future through the present into the past.

If one thinks of time in terms of motion, than its direction becomes relative; are we sliding by it, or is it sliding by us? That is why the concept of two types of time, incident and lateral, is handy. Incident time is existence or persistence; it has no past or future, only "now". The "now" dimension of an object is every bit as solid as its dimensions of length, width, and depth; your just not used to thinking of it that way, which is why you find it hard to believe.

Lateral time is what we normally think of as "time"; it is the time of events and of memory. Without motion of inertial mass, lateral time ceases to exist. It is memory that makes us aware of lateral time expressed in the motion of matter. Each change of position of the center of inertial mass or spin is lateral time being expressed. If the displacement is large enough, that change may register on our sensory system and become part of our memory. We are aware of the past from memory and familiar things about us, but the present keeps melting into the future. As this happens, the remembered past grows longer and larger while our present still lasts only a fraction of an instant before we find ourselves in the near-future, which immediately becomes our present, and just as fast, slides into the past. As a result, our memory consists of only past events; there is no future or present time represented in the memory. That is why it is so difficult to understand that the past, like the future, does not exist in physical reality; our memories seem so "real" in the present that it's not an easy thing to see that memory is also abstract and must go into the 5th dimension.

Just as matter persists in incident time and is sliding through lateral time, it is also sliding through space. An object, because it is moving (and all inertial mass is moving) it is only in a specific space for an instant before it is sliding into another part of space. The earth is moving yearly about the Sun as it spins daily on its axis; the whole solar system is embedded in an arm of our galaxy which is itself slowly turning in space. And the entire galaxy is rushing through space, away from other galaxies. So you can see, an object on the earth's surface has at least 4 different, major, motion vectors to its direction of travel, even if it is a "motionless" mountain; its place, in both space and time, is changing continuously!

Matter was generally considered to exist in 3 states, solid, liquid and gas, before the end of the 19th century. In the early 20th century, it slowly became apparent that 99% of the observed universe was in another state - the plasma state. It is a kind of disembodied state where there are no elements as we know them. The enormous thermo-nuclear energy of the stars rip ordinary atomic structure into a homogenized mix of separate protons, neutrons and electrons - a super-heated mix called plasma. The stars and galaxies are matter in this plasma state. Solids and liquids, or even elements higher than Calcium, are in fact extremely rare. With the exception of meteors, comets, and dwarf or neutron stars, there is no other significant accretion of a solid or a liquid outside the solar system. In any case, plasma is now considered as a state of matter; so we have 4 states of matter located in 4 dimensions of space / time.

Mass and energy are interchangeable but, can be neither created nor destroyed. The laws of motion, action / reaction equivalence; the conservation laws of mass, inertia, momentum, energy, etc. The fact that every effect is preceded by its cause.

The key piece of information to understanding it all, and all at once, is "order". If we make the simple assumption that there was a beginning (any one you like, take your pick) to the universe, and that that "cause" resulted in a clean, unbroken chain of action = reaction, cause - effect - cause - etc..., and mass/energy equivalence right up to the present moment; then to me, that means "order". The enormous size, age and complexity do not negate the simplicity of its operational constraints. With the advantage of 2000 years of "hind-sight", we can begin to see that wherever man has investigated any part of the natural world (NOT including himself), he has always found order. And the closer his look or the deeper his probe, he has always found another layer of order. After 2000 years of continuous (well, almost continuous) discoveries, I think we have been cautious to a fault. Given that we exclude all life forms, can we not now say, with great confidence, "there is NO chaos in the universe!" In the swirling mass of the hottest star all action and reaction is a function of cause giving birth to effect. There is not an atom, or a part of an atom, located but where it should be as a result of a previous action. Every particle of matter and quantum of energy is precisely where it HAS to be. The universe is unfolding as it should.

Billiards is often used to help illustrate the causal nature of what is going on in the universe as a whole. We shall continue the tradition, but extend the analog somewhat, in order for us to get a better idea of how man interacts with the game.

The cue-ball is white and all the object balls are colored or numbered so we can tell which is which. The cue-ball is struck with a cue-stick and driven against the object balls, which then move in accordance with fairly well understood laws of action / reaction, transfer of energy or force, conservation of linear and angular momentum, heat of impact or friction, etc., etc. A high speed camera records the action for later review. On the break, the balls roll every which way on the 2 dimensional surfaces, bouncing off each other and the table's cushioned edge, slowly loosing momentum until they all come to a halt. No one can predict the final resting place of all the balls.

At first sight the motion may be said to be random; but if we now playback in slow motion, our camera's view of the activity, we can see that all the apparent random motions clearly result from specific ball-to-ball and ball-to-cushion interaction. We know from previous experiments in dynamics that friction is what brings everything to a halt, and that the whole apparatus has become imperceptibly warmer because of the conversion of kinetic energy to heat-energy (two motions, but measured differently). Upon frame by frame study of the film, we can see that the motion and final resting place of any one ball is exactly as it should be. Random motion and chaos were an illusion! There was no point in time that a single ball was anywhere other than the place it should be, as mediated by the cause and effect nature of action verses reaction. Indeed, analyses shows, that it could be in no other place; it HAS to be where it is. Not approximately; but precisely, where it is.

Given the exact parameters of the mass and elasticity of the balls, the mass, elasticity and acceleration embodied in the cue stick, all dimensions and coefficients of friction, resilience of the cushions, density, humidity, temperature and pressure of the air, the gravity ... well, you get the idea; 19th century science was so brash as to declare it could predict the final resting place of each ball. All they needed were all the facts.

Today, science knows measurements that fine and that accurate cannot be made without affecting the progress of the action being observed. We can know a particles' position or we can know its velocity, but we cannot know both parameters at once for the same particle. For man, the final resting place of all the balls will forever remain indeterminate - a small mystery of the future that will resolve itself as kinetic energy of motion translates into distributed heat and stillness - total entropy.

Do not lose sight of the critical fact being outlined; the observed action / reaction is the direct result of cause / effect operations. There was and is no randomness or chaos - all is order. As we try for finer and finer measurements of detail, our own measurements begin to interfere with the "natural order" and our own measuring technique begins to enter the final equations. For the atomic physicist this is a maddening phenomenon that blurs every aspect of his view of "ultimate particles". But for me, this is exciting verification that man is indeed an intrinsic part of the universe - we are interacting with it at very fundamental levels. It also provides the awesome spectacle of a universe slowly becoming aware of itself.

Nineteenth century science had the view that, given all relevant data, the future is knowable. We still agree with the logic, but now recognize that the pre-condition for the forecast is unavailable to us. Thus the future is, and forever will be, unknowable. Is it probable and somewhat predictable - yes; knowable no. But let's take the game a bit further and point out that the analogy freezes an event in one space/time frame. The billiard table didn't appear by magic. Somebody made it. Then somebody moved it into the billiard hall. Somebody had to make the balls and the cue stick; the holders for the balls and cue-sticks; the building that housed the billiard hall. And somebody had to give birth to all those people who made up the billiard game analogy.

An incredibly complex chain of cause and effect had to take place throughout this planet and moving up out of the distant past, to the time and the place of the game being played. A sequence of apparently unrelated events were occurring in past time and in separate spaces, on parallel time lines, that converged on our billiard hall and brought table, ball, player and observer into one harmonious whole. It came about by cause and effect of forces on matter; some too subtle to be detectable, but still identifiable and imaginable in the over-all view of things. And the conclusion that I get is that things are as they are and could not be any other way; that any sequence of events is orchestrated by a chorus of laws working in harmony. No one law is more controlling or dominant than any other; all are equal and none conflict. Everything is precisely as it has to be because it came about by a sequence that cannot fail. If any cause or any effect should happen to miss-fire, the entire universe would halt at that instant. Right now, at this instant, throughout the entire universe, everything that "is" exists because of a cause or event that just now slid into the past; -AND- everything, right-now, is connected by a web of cause and event that stretches back, unbroken, through 15 billion years to the very first event. A singularity in itself. The creation of the universe. You are not here by accident.

PERSPECTIVES

Perspective is the English word-tag, or sound-pattern, used to suggest that the way we understand things is dependent on how we view them. A man in a valley has a different "sense" of the world than a man on a mountain. The world is the same for both, but each has a different comprehension of what it is and what it means, because each is limited to a different environment. The man on a plateau, mid-way between the extremes, will have a view that is often a blending of the two; a better understanding of the world because he can be aware of the extremes on either side of his position.

While the extreme views can be aware of the plateau man, they may be completely ignorant of each other. The sensory high-low limits of man's nervous system places his comprehensive apparatus, the brain, exactly at the center of his perceived universe. Over the centuries this memory center has manipulated its limited intellectual control over the rest of the bodily organs, to construct instruments that can extend the natural limitations of its sensors.

The first such devise was the magnifying glass that allowed failing eyes, in candle-lit rooms, to see again the written or printed script. Eye glasses became the rage of Europe about the same time that the telescope/microscope was invented. Did you ever think that the telescope and microscope are exactly the same thing; or that the difference between the two is totally dependent on which way you look through it! The ancient ones thought that we saw things as a result of some kind of ray that emerged from the eye - just as a child thinks today, as its brain struggles to orient the body to its environment. The child knows nothing of the physics of light and optical laws, or that vision is actually taking place inside the brain. When the child closes its eye lids, in average light, there is the distinct impression that the eye can still see the back of the eye lid. For the ancient ones and a child this is proof enough that the rays responsible for sight are emanating from the eye itself. But let's get back to perspective.

The first two lens instruments acted as a low power microscope if the eye were placed near the large lens and as a low power telescope if the eye were placed near the small lens! When the light being viewed is traveling from the small lens to the large lens, it is being diverged. Because the light is coming from a small source, as it is spread out its intensity per unit area is decreased. Therefore, in order to get enough light to stimulate the retina, the specimen being viewed must be very brightly illuminated with increasing magnification. Early instruments often barbecued the cells being viewed and probably contributed to the frantic activity that so delighted the novice observer. When the eye is placed next to the small lens and the instrument is directed at a distant object, the incoming light rays, are being converged and the image seen appears much brighter and the object much closer. When used as a telescope, light is being collected and stars too faint to activate the retina normally, may now be seen. The sun is ever present in mans view of the world - the temptation to have a good look at it is almost irresistible. Many an early observer, in times both past and present, learned too late the danger of gazing at its fiery face. The suns focused image will instantly cook a dead spot on the retinas sensitive fovea - it will not recover - the eye will be permanently blind in the very center of the visual field. No young person should ever be given free access to any telescope or binoculars during daylight hours.

With increasing knowledge of how to manipulate light, the two uses of the same instrument soon diverged into two different instruments that then became increasingly modified to enhance the principle purpose of each device; i.e., a microscope is crafted to diverge light with maximum resolution and minimum distortion a telescope is crafted to converge light for maximum resolution with minimum distortion.

One should not assume that by merely looking through one of these instruments, one immediately "views" another world. Vision is a learning process - it takes time and it takes repetition. Detecting is what the eye does - it senses an image and transmits simultaneously, on hundreds of separate nerve fibers, a separate coded response-signal in each separate fiber. The visual cortex of the brain then compares the patterns of the received code with remembered previous patterns, and creates the sensation we call vision. Without some remembered pattern for comparison and matching, we do not understand what the eye sees - the vision is indistinct. We can "see" the specimen quite clearly but with no similar images stored in the "visual pattern" memory banks we cannot make a comparison, let alone a match. The visual cortex finds itself at a new beginning again; it has to learn to "see" all over again, in terms of looking at and understanding what these new images (light-patterns) mean. It takes many months of "looking" before a new micro or telescopic series of light patterns are stored in the memory and the brain slowly learns to have vision when the eye peeps through optical image makers. We, (the brain-eye), "learn" to see through these instruments, and it is that learning that becomes knowledge and then understanding, and separates (usually) the professional from the novice. Modern students are unfortunately denied this invaluable insight into their own learning modes because they are inundated with accurate drawings and color photographs of what they are about to see. They have already stored pages of pictures and notes in their memories before looking into the eye-piece. Most see nothing odd. They have been cheated of the excitement and wonder that greets the mature brain that suddenly begins to receive new patterns in the blip-code from its sensors. Early investigators had no such foresight, so each time they changed the specimen slide they were treated to a visual feast and more marvels of fact than could ever be supposed by the most fertile imagination. It took hundreds of years for mans collective brain to begin to understand via the linguistic code, what its collective eye was seeing.

At the beginning of the 20th century there were few structural hints that either instrument had a common ancestor or that both was still doing essentially the same thing with light and that it was strictly "perspective" that determined what we saw through either. By the 1950's the human eye itself had been replaced by other mechanical sensors on both telescope and microscope as the brain peered ever further beyond the upper and lower limits of its natural light sensor. Also, both instruments had reached their practical limits of resolution and are now being supplemented (not replaced) by radio telescopes and electron-microscopes to continue our perceptual extension.

The early micro/tele/scope gives us a chance to put man in perspective with the universe he is sensing. Anything smaller than can be seen by the human eye is microscopic. Any thing too far away to be resolved into a shape by the unaided human eye is macroscopic. In other words, any thing which does not register as a change on our natural sensors may be thought of as being part of the microscopic (very small) or macroscopic (very large or distant) universe in which man's mesoscopic (middle size) world is embedded. Unless our natural sensors are activated, either directly or indirectly, we can have no conscious knowledge of any event. The mesoscopic world is defined by the detectable changes that occur within the stimuli that activate our natural, unaided sensors.

For 40 thousand years mans intellect has been limited to his mesoscopic world. For barely four hundred years he has begun to extend his sensory perception with hard facts that fly in the face of belief systems rooted in centuries of ignorance and irrational fear. For barely one hundred years he has come to understand his animal nature. For barely thirty years he has come to know that his body is the colony of a single fertilized cell; we are still struggling to understand the implications of that fact. Its rational staggers the imagination.

At the close of the 1800's man was becoming aware that all his systems of reference were arbitrary assignments that had relevance only through international agreement. There was no absolute unit of length or mass or time. Even absolute "0" of temperature was suspect and later proved not to be "absolute" when a temperature lower than that was demonstrated, theoretically at least, by reductions in the spin of the atomic nucleus of solid helium. The absolute velocity of light in a vacuum seemed secure, but velocity is time X distance and both these are arbitrary. Also, relativity shows length compression and time dilation with increase in either velocity or mass. Besides that, we don't know what light "is". The natural laws of material interaction in man's mesoscopic world were seen to be inadequate to account for phenomena being observed in the macro and microscopic worlds; we had no way to account for the energy being delivered by our sun and no explanation as to how a plant used that energy here on earth. New understandings were not long in coming, but they revealed more levels of order to material interaction and new laws that controlled those interactions. The laws governing gases, liquids, solids and gross mechanical laws of the mesoscopic world gave way to the microscopic laws governing molecular and atomic interactions. Chemical laws mediated the material interactions as modified by permeable membranes. Examples are osmosis, colloidal states, enzyme catalyzers and hormones at the cellular level of life. Gravity or mechanical leverage have no role to play within the membrane of a single cell; these become effective only as a cell colony mass begins to be large enough to impinge on the mesoscopic world. The cell is produced from the molecules of compounds that are constructed by the natural valance bonds that can exist between the atoms of different elements. Further assembly of molecules and atoms into amino and nucleotide acids is determined by the order of the nucleotides strung out on the DNA molecule that is involved in reproducing the cell. Hydrogen ion concentration in fluids (blood) is controlled by acid/base interchanges. Adhesion and cohesion between molecules is barely detectable in our world but is a powerful force in the microscopic world. Surface tension of water is for us a curiosity; for a small house-fly, surface tension is a death trap and small insects that need water to drink are equipped with a special feeding tube that allows them to stand well back from the waters edge.

All living things are built up from materials in a colloidal state. This is a stable condition where particles do not settle out of a solvent, but remain diffused throughout the medium as tiny microscopic particles, due partly to their continuous movement but mainly because of the small electric charge (either all positive or all negative) carried by each particle. The continuous movement - called Brownian motion - was cause for much debate when initially noticed, but is now known to be caused by the kinetic energy of motion (heat) of the molecules making up the mass of the colloid. The tiny particles are kept separated from each other by their like electric charge and thus tend to distribute themselves evenly throughout the liquid - much as a gas expands to fill its container. The Brownian movement is called "random" motion, but is of the same nature as the "random" motion of billiard balls. That is, when all the parameters of material interaction are known and considered then no effect is a random event, but is a direct result of its preceding cause. The degree of "randomness" we see in everyday events is inversely proportional to our knowledge of the circumstances. Or to put it another way, the more we come to know about our world, the less random does it become; chaos is the view of ignorance.

I am looking out at reality through the lattice-word sphere and all the word "meanings" are in here with "me". Hopefully you will appreciate that ones' view is largely determined by ones' vantage point. The external environment of the world and the internal environment of my body are outside the sphere of words. The "words" are the last flicker of physical reality; the final physical barrier between reality and abstraction; between material existence and immaterial non-existence; between brain and mind. The sound patterns of the words that make-up the lattice-work sphere are connected to the web of nerve fibers that provide the coded information streaming in from the physical world.

Lets have a quick peek; 4 billion years back in time, courtesy of that wonder of wonders, language.

The earth is a sphere, 3rd planet from the Sun, about which it revolves once each year. It rotates on its axis once each day, 365 times for each one revolution about the Sun. Its axis of rotation is tilted 23 ½ degrees to the plane of its solar orbit and this gives us the seasons. It has one large moon that, along with the Sun, are said to cause tides on the ocean shores. There are two low tides and two high tides each day. The matter of the earth is made up of elements which have formed into compounds. These may seem to be trivial truths, but they are all absolutely essential for what is to come - life. There is no stable element detectable in the universe that is not present on earth, but many of the heavier elements and most compounds on earth have not been detected outside the solar system. The matter on earth exists in solid, liquid and gaseous states which are mainly determined by temperature and marginally affected by pressure. The plasma state on earth is very rare and only transitory when it does manifest itself: a strong lightening stroke is about as close as our environment will let it get, naturally; it's not something you'd like in your back yard.

The real plasma state of matter had never been closer to earth than about 93 million miles, until July 16/1945. On that date, near Alamogordo, N.M., USA, at 5:30 AM local time, it appeared briefly and melted the desert sand into a ragged glass bowl, of about 1000 yards in diameter. On Aug. 6 and 9 of that same year the 1st state of matter sputtered again over Hiroshima and Nagasaki, Japan. It has been flickering sporadically about our precious globe ever since; as the 5th state of matter (life) played with the 1st state of matter (Plasma). Will the child with the matches' burn down his own home? We can only wait and see.

Although most of the elements that make up the earth (and you) were forged in the pulse of a Super-Nova, the compounds made from these elemental atoms were assembled here, in the solar system and on earth itself. For example, hydrogen and oxygen are both gasses. These two gasses can combine in a measured way to produce a liquid, water! The liquid is totally different from the two gasses that make it up and there is no way of predicting what will result when we bring two or more pure elements together for the first time, under given conditions of temperature and pressure.

On earth, the three states are generally very stable because the planet's temperature and pressure are very stable. Fluctuation between states is rare and usually temporary. The compound water is a spectacular exception; it fluctuates between its liquid and gas state daily, and between liquid and solid seasonally. Clouds of water vapor are common in the atmosphere which is quite thin and consists mainly of nitrogen and methane gas (oxygen comes later). Fifty percent of the atmosphere's total mass is below about 3 miles, and pressure at sea-level is about 15 1b per sq. in. The planets surface area is three-quarters water and one-quarter scattered land masses of very low level. Condensation from clouds tends to be both regional and seasonal; because much of the rainfall is over the oceans, the land surface is rather arid. There is very little precipitation at either pole. Changes in the planets land topography, or ratios between the solid, liquid and gas constituents tend to be very slow, requiring millions of years. The occasional volcanic eruption is rare and its effects, generally, very local.

On the whole, it's a rather quiet place; not much happening; not what you expected at all. Sorry. But you see, this an incubator; something very fragile and wonderful is about to come into existence here – life, the fifth state of matter, is just beyond the next dawn. We will not stay to watch its birth; there are many theories you can peruse in other books. But we will have a quick look about while we're here.

We are near a continental coast where a large river is depositing its load of eroded land into an estuary. It is raining but there are breaks in the heavy cloud cover, where sunlight pours through to brighten the bleak sea and landscape. There are no plants or animals. No grass or trees crowd the river's muddy banks - there is no soil yet, just sterile sand and mud and rock. The land is a wet jumble of rock, glistening in the subdued light. No flowers bloom in this quiet place; no wing of bird or insect disturbs the silent air. In the sea, no fish or plankton float; the water is crystal clear out beyond the river's mouth. Everything is ready; waiting.

Gravity holds the air and water to the earth's face and pulls the struggling river out of the land and into the sea. The liquid water tries to escape by changing into a vapor and rising into the atmosphere, but decreasing pressure and temperature force it back into the liquid state and it falls weeping to the surface. In the process, it absorbed heat from the ocean and released heat to the atmosphere; by using the air's density gradient, it converted potential energy of the ocean to kinetic energy of the rain-drop and river. In the mountains, the drop of liquid may become a chisel of ice that can split the toughest rock. The energy of the Sun is the main source of power. Its presence (day) and absence (night) drives the mechanical inter-actions of matter on the earth's surface and in its oceans of air and water. A one percent increase in radiant energy and the earth would be a dry, airless cinder; a one percent decrease and earth would be a frozen snowball.

The reason I have brought you back to a time just before life is not to show what is here; it is what isn't here that has significance to the understanding of "self" in particular, and life in general. I have been writing about how the light glistens on the rock but that is silly poetic license; there is no "light" in this place! The electromagnetic waves are here but the sensory apparatus of eye and brain that converts it to "light" has not yet evolved. There is no light here even though the physical phenomena needed to produce it are all around us! What we call light is a very small part of a very large spectrum of electromagnetic energy that extends from very long waves of low frequency radio, smoothly up the electromagnetic scale to very short waves of very high frequency (ultra-violet and cosmic rays). The universe doesn't make any qualitative judgments about its products or processes; it doesn't produce light or color - just the interplay of energy and matter. Only man chooses to call a particular part of the spectrum "light"; and only he does so (in English, remember) because his eye is sensitive to that narrow band of frequency, and signals the brain to say it is being stimulated - and some part of the brain says, ah yes, "light". But he learned that word-tag, that sound-pattern, through his ear / brain / throat.

There is no sound here either! No sensor to react to the atmospheric rarefactions and compressions that are reverberating from waves crashing on the beach; the ear has not yet evolved. All the physical elements are there, ready to be heard, but there is no sensor to detect them and no brain to interpret that stimulation and say, ah yes, "sound". There are no "odors" or "tastes" either, for lack of a sensor and a brain. If we could, "feel" the breeze blowing in from the sea, we could not tell if it were "hot" or "cold", "soft" or "hard". Sensory effects do not exist yet because the animal brain that gives expression to these "qualities" has not yet come to give meaning (word-tags) and purpose to those things it detects. There is no up or down, left or right, far or near, because these are subjective, and the object of that subjectivity is yet to come. There is no positive or negative, no soft or hard, no capacity or density, because these are relative things and the thing that will do the comparing is 4 billion years into the future. Love and hate, fear and shame, pride and conceit are all emotions and do not exist here; they too await the coming. Freedom and slavery, right and wrong, good and bad, religion, art, music, mathematics, politics, economy, language are all abstract concepts, and these also are not here in the time before life. They must await the coming of the great one, the only one.

I hope you can see that before life began the universe was relatively simple - and it had order; no chaos existed. It was a bit on the large side to be sure, but basically, quite simple. Cause and effect (not love and hate) mediated by natural laws, as expressed on material matter, took care of everything and made sure that everything had its place. Nothing was where it could not be and order and sequence rule supreme. From this time, just before life, an unbroken chain of cause/effect events stretches back to the very beginning; not a single atom or quantum of energy is anywhere but where it must be.

The bi-peddle gait of our hairless body, with its opposable thumbs, would be hard pressed to secure us a place at the feeding trough without that most peculiar anomaly of the brain that directs it; "thinking" with abstract symbols.

Ours is not the only brain that is doing this, but so far, it is doing it better than any other. To understand how and why the brain is "thinking", we have to first understand what "life" is, and how the 5th dimension (the "mind" if you like), came to be located in it. So let's have a peek at "life".

Chapter 5
Life: *The 5ᵗʰ State of Matter and the 5ᵗʰ Dimension of Mind*

The 5ᵗʰ State of Matter. Three and a half billion years ago and life proliferates in the oceans and is beginning to invade the fresh waters flowing from the land, in the deltas of rivers. There is still no life form higher than the single cell, but these many different kinds of cells are beginning to stabilize into colonies by clinging to floating debris and the shores of land masses. Colonization is also being promoted by the variation of conditions in separate localities and competition from nearby relatives.

Cells are made mainly from elements of hydrogen, oxygen, nitrogen and carbon which then combine naturally into molecules of various composition and structure called nucleotides and amino acids. Whether "life" begins with the DNA made from the nucleotides or when the amino acids are used to construct a nebulous membrane of protein about its fragile cytoplasmic contents, we're not sure. The cell has been arbitrarily assigned as the unit of life.

Cars, boats and airplanes are mainly made from elements of iron, carbon, copper and aluminum which combine unnaturally (i.e. under mans control) into various materials that man then works into different fasteners and parts that, when properly assembled, make a transportation unit; such as a train. All these products are artifacts - made by man; the cell is "natural" - made by nature. But since any animal is an assemblage of co-operative organs which are in turn colonies of co-operative cells - and the cells are made by nature - would it not be fair to say that the artifacts of man are no less natural to the world than is man himself? Is the stick and mud dam that Neolithic man first placed across a small creek any less natural than the stick and mud dam of the Neolithic beaver?

A small sub-group of humans, in terms of the English language, has come to use a particular set of sound patterns for audible and written communications. The sound pattern used to express the word-tags for the physical states of matter are "plasma, gas, liquid, & solid". Each of these words is used to represent the main characteristic of any piece of matter under given conditions of temperature, pressure and density. We are going to add a 5th state to material existence because, just as the other four states have characteristics exclusive to their temperature, pressure and density range, the 5th state has its own unique set of characteristics determined by these same variables. We will give this 5th state of matter the word-tag "life". For those who insist that this word is already in use, let me reassure you that we are only going to give added meaning and understanding by considering "life" as a state, the 5th state, of matter. The basic form of the 5th state is the cell, in all forms of plant and animal species.

The 5th state of matter, life, is no less dependent on temperature, pressure and density than any other state. The mean temperature on earth to-day is about 16 deg C, and it would not have been more than a few degrees higher, when the first cells are believed to have formed. Above 45 deg C, the valance bonds of the tertiary protein structure are over-come by the mechanical motion (heat) of the environment - they begin to break apart - melt. Below about 0 degrees C, the mechanical motion (heat) is too low to maintain the gentle molecular mixing necessary to bring the various elements and molecules together for the valance bond to bind - the mix begins to gel. Because of this temperature dependency, all forms of successful life have developed strategies to minimize the effects of natural temperature variation. Evolution in multi-cell plants and animals will develop an enormous range of diverse methods of stabilizing their internal temperatures. But for now, these simple cells can only respond to unfavorable external temperatures by "moving" to cooler or warmer locations. The same may be said for conditions of salinity, acidity, pressure, turbulence, light intensity, or any other influence prejudicial to its chemical processes. One of the prime attributes of a living cell is its motility; the ability to move in a determined manner.

Modern biology regards the cell as the unit of life but finds great difficulty in defining life as a "thing", because of course it is a process, not a thing. Arguments ensue over whether a virus is alive or not because of its method of reproduction. It has to penetrate a host cell and then it makes the host cell's reproductive facilities make copies of the invading virus. It is the host cell that is reproducing the virus bodies, not the virus itself dividing.

Modern man equates "life" with consciousness and awareness that is somehow rooted in, and part of, his physical cellular body. The brain-dead body is not aware of and cannot respond to the stimuli being detected by its still active sensors. For man, "life" without conscious awareness of self is no life at all - it has no purpose or meaning. Defining "life" is similar to the legal problems of controlling pornography in society; we might not be able to define it, but we know what it is when we see it! The problem is one of semantics or nomenclature and the relationship between the physical and mental "you". It is a problem of language. We need a new word, or expression, to help us understand the new information we have gathered about our world. Let's re-arrange a few words in our lattice-word sphere and put a new meaning into our 5th dimension. Let's use the word "life" to mean the physical process of certain materials that only occurs under particular conditions of temperature and pressure (molecular motion). Let's call that physical reality of material process, the 5th state of matter.

Life is not a "thing" or magic spark - it is a special material process, mediated by natural laws of material interaction with time. It eventually becomes conscious of its process and then aware of its "being". It is a very, very special state of matter. Let us pay due accord to its marvels. Let's honor its special status in the material reality of the universe. Let us use the power it has bequeathed to man - the power of language. Let's give it a name - the 5th state of matter. Let us understand that the universe is unfolding as it should and that not a particle of matter or a quantum of energy is anywhere but where it must be due to the cause that just now preceded it. Life persists and reproduces in two mainly symbiotic groups, animals and plants.

The main physical distinction of the 5th state of matter, from the other four states, is that it is expressed in aggregates of materials in discreet units, called a cell that reproduces itself and may move about with no apparent outside force acting on it. Just as the other four states blend into each other, so the cell blurs from inanimate to animate; animals and plants.

Life is a material process and is no more (or less) magical than the elements, compounds and laws of matter that make up the body of the cell. It is all perfectly natural and adheres to the same basic laws that mediate any part of the universe. That "life" has come into existence on the third planet from our sun should not be viewed as accidental or a miracle just because we don't presently know every little detail about its appearance.

It has been here over three billion years and we have only been able to examine it factually for about forty years; since the electron microscope. Individual animals and plants that can be seen with the naked eye appeared only 600 million years ago. The store of factual information is growing faster than we can assimilate it; understanding takes time.

The ancient ones thought human life was so special and complex that it could not have come about naturally on this harsh earth but required the superior mind and power of a divine creator. The factual knowledge of evolution in fossils and of 20th century biology in comparative anatomy and embryology, biochemistry and molecular biology, sways not the true believer who is emotionally locked into the 10th century. Even many of today's scientists, who after all are only human themselves, cannot shake man's narcissistic mantle, and speculate that life (being so special) must have come to earth (this terrible place) in a meteorite, or perhaps from refuse discarded by some ancient astronaut. The plain truth is that if we can ignore for a moment our incredible infatuation with how wonderful we are; these speculations of aliens, meteorites and old lunch-boxes are not needed in face of the growing, factual knowledge of how the various amino acids formed into their protein strands.

To the inanimate world, time, like everything else, means nothing at all. To the living world, it is as essential as temperature and pressure or food and drink. Lateral time came into existence when the very first cell persisting in incident time, began to rotate its substance about its center of mass. The perception of lateral time has come into existence only with the 5th state of matter, and its content of the 5th dimension of mind with memory.

All life forms, single cell or multi-cell, plant or animal, have timed cycles of various activities; moving, feeding, resting, breathing, drinking, reproducing, eliminating waste, growth, etc. All of these activities are timed by the individual metabolic rate and synchronize the external and internal environments of the life form.

Many of these activities are linked to the cyclical motions of our planet on a daily, monthly, seasonal or yearly schedule. Many land animals have an ancestral aquatic tie that is synchronized with the periodic tides of the oceans, which are in turn linked in part to the motions of the moon and apparent motion of the sun. The human female has an average 28 day fertility cycle which may have been established in the distant past with lunar phenomena, tides. Time sense emerged, long before the first true cell, from an underlying precondition of "life" itself. It is obvious that, in the warm ocean soup of pre-life amino acids, the casual chains of poly-peptides and proteins first assembled would be quickly knocked apart again by the thermal-molecular activity that exceeded the binding strength of chemical valance bonds. The first DNA chain that managed to duplicate itself was determined by the time between sustained formation and actual replication. That time interval would have been a function of molecular activity; which is motion or energy that we refer to as temperature. So time, in a sense, may be "breade in the flesh" as a function of heat; and as every connoisseur of good soup knows, the temperature is just as important as the ingredients.

Three and a half billion years ago, the oceans are a primordial soup of organic molecules that has yielded up a literal feast of single cells. The first cellular organisms produced by the life process were probably bacteria and blue-green algae. Once the DNA molecules began to stabilize in the slowly cooling ocean, the bacterial activity must have been spectacular. Some bacteria can multiply so rapidly, that in just one day of growth, a single cell may reproduce into two million cells - their uninhibited growth is explosive.

The only reason we are not up to our necks in these little critters is because they quickly gobble-up their own food supply or die in their own excremental pollution. Isn't it comforting to have human intelligence and the free-will that allows mankind the choices to avoid over-population, exceeding our own food supply, or poisoning our own environment? Bacteria are so stupid! After a few hundred million years of repeated population crashes, some bacteria developed a method of getting energy from light, called photosynthesis that reduced their dependency on the energy supplied by chemosynthesis of metabolizing the hydro-carbon molecules of their ingested food supply.

The appearance of blue-green algae about 800 million years after the life process began marks the precursor of the world we will know in the 20th century; they were probably the first organisms that extracted hydrogen from water molecules and threw away, as waste, the oxygen gas that is essential to animal life as we know it today. Actual protozoan, or "pre-animal" cells, won't develop for about another 800 million years, but here, three and a half billion years before the 20th century, cells have already taken on the main characteristics that are the foundation of all plant and animal activity: self preservation and reproduction.

We will recall these two activities later on because they explain about 99% of what mankind does and why he does it. For now, two billion years before man comes into the scene, I would just like you to consider these activities as two separate but related programs of the 5th state of matter. They are programs because each individual cell, of each species of cells, has its own unique sequences of ordered process that expresses each of the two activities. Program one is self-preservation; used in the maintenance of the individual. Program two is reproduction; used in the maintenance of the species. These two programs are almost equal in terms of compulsion, and are very much the opposite sides of the single coin of preservation.

Because "life" is a process and survival is the process extended, survival is the name of the game of life. The two menus of programmed activity drive the individual cell into behavioral sequences that promote the twin goals of individual survival and of species survival. These programs are not elective; they are compulsive drives to specific behavior honed to perfection by billions of years of precision "environment versus cell" selection, i.e.: evolution. These two programs extend, unabated, into the future multi-cell animals, including man. .

The process of life is chemical. Various materials combine with valance bonds to make up the compound substances that make up the organelles, cytoplasm, nucleus, contents and membranes of the cell as a whole. Chemical symbols (messages) are nature's way of controlling a cell's interaction with its environment, which includes other cells. As cells began to specialize and group, to become multi-cell individuals floating in a watery world, chemicals continued to mediate the interaction of various cells and organs "within" the individual.

Some chemicals were also useful externally for inter-communication between the separate individuals of the same species. For the multi-cell plants and animals there were now two environments; the internal one enveloped by their skin, and the larger external environment in which they floated. So long as organisms remained in water, chemical symbols or messages remained the principle control vector of natural selection in both internal and external environmental adaptation. That is, cells and multi-cell animals could receive chemical messages from potential food, friend or foe, mate or rival; or send a chemical message that could potentially repel enemies or attract mates.

When the organisms (first plants and then animals) moved onto land, the effectiveness of chemical messages in the external environment was drastically reduced due to the great difference in density between water and air and the mechanical difference between the liquid and gaseous states. Air is too thin to carry the large chemical molecules that are only stable in a liquid environment. But air can carry disturbances of pressure, compression and rarefaction - sound waves.

Plants have not developed any audio sensitivity. They have been able to adjust their life-style with only minor adaptations for stronger stems and modified pollination and seed distribution. They are not regarded as great communicators. For animals, sound sensors could be developed, by natural selection of pressure-organ modification, or re-using gill structures no longer needed on land. Without water to carry the chemical symbols (information), through the external environment between individuals of a species, sound symbols (information) became a working alternative.

Audio symbols, words, can be very powerful stimulators and considerably more diverse than chemical stimulators. What words lack in direct drive they more than make up for in diversity and subtlety. Audio symbols will become the evolutionary chosen method of communication through the external environment, between the higher animals; just as chemicals are for inter-cell communications (hormones, etc.) in the internal environment of all multi-cell animal and plant organisms.

Life is "process" of material and not a "thing" in itself. It is a temperature controlled chemical activity that leads to a particular arrangement of various elements, which then begin to combine such as to form discreet molecules of specific compounds of proteins, carbohydrates, fats, etc., in what was previously a homogenized soup of those same amino acid chemicals. Life is a sequential, cyclical continuity of a particular combination of molecular matter - it is the supreme expression of order; the total absence of chaos. There is no magical spark that suddenly causes life to appear in dead materials. It is very romantic to think so, but that is because we still do not understand the chemical process that results in the living cell. We are still trying to define life, let alone understand what "it" is.

By defining life as the 5th state of matter, we tie the chemical process that expresses it back into the natural world. If we are to understand life we must give it a material base in reality. If we accept that the states of matter are terms-of-convenience and not scientific definitions, we may feel a bit more comfortable with the idea that "life" is a state of matter (the 5th state) in general, and a process of material interaction in particular.

The reason that solids, liquids, etc. are concepts of convenience is that we now know that the vast majority of elements and compounds can only exist in these aggregates, depending on pressure and temperature. On earth, because of a very narrow temperature range, the material states appear to be very stable - almost constant. In fact, without this stable thermal condition life could not exist! Above 10,000 deg C all elements can exist only in the gaseous state, if at all. At about 5,000 deg C some of the heavier elements begin to condense into liquids. At about 500 deg C most of our familiar solids (iron, copper, stone) are here as solids, but others (lead, tin) are still liquid. At 100 deg C all the familiar solids are here but the only familiar liquid is mercury; the compound water would still be a gaseous vapor. At 50 deg C we would see a slightly more familiar world in that some of the oceans would be starting to form; but it is still probably too hot for the living cell, the 5th state of matter, to begin to form. At 0 deg C land water would begin to crystallize and oceans would be starting to gel; any life that had developed would be no longer tenable (Human core temp, is about 37 deg C; a sustained core temp, of 5 deg C above or below the norm, for more than a day, will usually cause unconsciousness and irreparable damage to the brain.)

At -50 deg C mercury is a solid bead in the thermometer and chlorine is getting ready to solidify. At -200 deg C oxygen and nitrogen are liquids and at -250 deg C, oxygen and nitrogen have solidified and hydrogen is a liquid. At -270 deg C hydrogen has solidified and helium is the last liquid state in the universe - everything else is solid, and gas and plasmas are only memories. At -272.2 deg C and a pressure of 26 atmospheres, helium enters its solid state. Absolute 0, where only the solid state of matter can exist, is considered to be about -273.16 deg C; where molecular vibration ceases.

Just as the different materials vary their states with pressure and temperature, the natural laws expressed by these states and materials come into play during the solid, liquid and gas phases. In the plasma state, the natural laws for that material phase are for all intents, unknown. We believe the strong and weak forces are operating to allow proton and neutron existence, but how they work is not understood. The gas state begins to express qualities like volume, density, compression, adsorption, and buoyancy, molecular motion as heat and pressure, inertia and expanding to fill the space of its container. Both gas and liquids are considered as fluids, dynamically speaking. The liquid state is considered to be only slightly compressible and, in addition to the gas qualities, viscosity, surface tension, absorption, molecular stability etc., it conforms to the shape of its container. The solid state is characterized by rigidity, impenetrable and crystalline structure to its molecular arrangement.

There are at least 92 natural elements and millions of different compounds are constructed from these elements in the narrow energy band of our planet earth. Many of these materials are not only temperature dependent but, in some very important instances, pressure and density dependent as well. Consider liquid water which is critical to the material process that has produced life. We all know that the liquid state of water is temperature dependent but few appreciate that it is pressure dependent as well. Without the atmosphere pressing against the vapor pressure of the oceans, they would be subject to rapid evaporation and then any fluid remaining would freeze solid due to the heat loss caused by the evaporation.

Water contracts with heat-loss, as do most materials, but at 3.98 deg C (this is also a standard density reference) water begins to expand as temperatures continue to drop; no other common material reverses its co-efficient of expansion as it approaches its solid state. This allows water the novelty of solidification from the surface down. Ice forms at its surface, not at the colder bottom where it contacts the land. Although the freezing and boiling points of pure water are used to establish the standard references on thermometers, these transition points are dependent on a sea-level air pressure of 750 mm. Water boils at a lower temperature and freezes at a higher temperature on a mountain top due to reduced atmospheric pressure; sea water doesn't start to freeze until well below 0 deg C because of its high salt content; which also makes sea water more dense then fresh water and helps to explain how water temperature in the ocean depths can be lower than 0 deg C.

Pure water does not always change its state on temperature cue; nor is ice always less dense than the liquid state. If water is not physically disturbed it may be super-cooled to 1 or 2 C deg below 0 before it will suddenly crystallize with great expansive force. If water is pressurized, up to say 20,000 atmospheres and the cooled, several varieties of ice can form, depending on pressure and temp., and all are more dense (they sink) than the liquid; six different ices are known, ice #2 is 12%, and ice #3 is 3% denser than water.

Pure water can be heated, if not agitated, to as high as 180 C deg before suddenly converting explosively into its gaseous vapor state. Steam at 100 C deg occupies a volume 1700 times greater than that of water at the same temperature. That is, at 100 c deg, 1 cc of water converts to 1700 cc of steam after absorbing 540 cal of heat, with no change in temperature. So you'd better know what your doing when playing with water in a closed container at temperatures over 100 C deg - you could blow your face off.

Hydrogen, oxygen volume ratio is 2 to 1, and oxygen, hydrogen weight ratio is 8 to 1. The single water molecule is two hydrogen atoms attached by electron valance bonds to one oxygen atom in an asymmetrical form; that is, lines extended from a point and through the centers of each hydrogen atom and the single oxygen atom would have a "Y" shape. This causes a small electrical dipole to exist - one end is slightly more negative (or positive) than the other end and causes the molecules to form up in groups of 3 oxygen atoms, with their attached 6 hydrogen atoms, which helps neutralize the individual dipoles.

The abnormally high heat of vaporization (540 calories absorbed per gram of water to convert to a vapor) and high heat of fusion (80 calories released per gram to convert to a solid) is believed due to the electrical dipole that is referred to as the hydrogen bond. The hydrogen bond is also used to explain waters "wetting" abilities, surface tension, and the 6 pointed radial structures of ice-crystals and snow flakes. Water in its liquid form represents an enormous heat-sink, or heat storage medium, that is mainly responsible for the temperature stability of our planet. In particular, at the upper (100 C) and lower (0 C) ends of our familiar temperature reference scale, the enormous amounts of heat energy stored in the hydrogen bond structure literally locks the Earths ambient temperature between these points. This release of heat in the fall and absorption of heat in the spring is responsible for the one month delay between celestial and "actual" seasons on earth. About 73% of the earth's surface is liquid water, which represents about 7% of earth mass. Water is unequalled by any other liquid in its ability to dissolve solids, other liquids, and gases.

The alchemists of the middle ages searched for the universal solvent without any thought of what they would keep it in once they found it. Today we know that water is as close as we are likely to get to the universal solvent. Also, many chemical reactions will only take place in the solvent medium of water - it is certainly the catalyst for the 5th state of matter; life. Photosynthesis could not take place in plants without the water molecule and its remarkable dipolar structure. In a plant, 6 molecules of water and 6 molecules of carbon dioxide are taken from the environment and, in the presence of light, a single molecule of 6 carbon sugar glucose is produced for food and 6 molecules of oxygen are dumped into the atmosphere. Man cannot live without oxygen and all the oxygen in the atmosphere has been produced by plants breaking up water molecules. All single cells can be seen to be tiny capsules of liquid. As plants and animals evolved they all entrained water within their bodies for the journey onto land. The cactus and lizard may appear as dry as dust, but if they are alive they have liquid water inside and are actively engaged in keeping it there.

The DNA and amino acids that combine in ordered sequence to make cells could not be realized without the solvent support medium of water. Indeed, it is understood the Hydrogen bond links the rungs of the helical ladder of life (DNA). If all this talk about water has made you a tad thirsty, give a wink and a nod to your next glass of water before you drink 'er down - it really is the nectar of the divine.

The Unit of the 5th State of Matter

The English word-tag "cell" is derived from the Latin word Cella, which means, "small room". The word-tag, as applied to prison-cell or battery-cell or the comb-cell of the honey-bee, can be thought of as small "compartments", each essentially the same. As applied to the 5th state of matter, early microscopic observations of living matter were based on plant tissue where cellulose walls of plant structure were the most prominent feature. These walled units were regarded as compartments or small rooms, and came to be called "cells". As facts accumulated into knowledge and then into understanding, it became apparent these cell-walls were in fact structures that were produced by, and separate from, the substance inside. The cell-wall material came to be called cellulose and the "stuff" inside came to be called a living cell. Initially, the cell was seen to be divided into two principle parts; a nucleus and a surrounding envelope of jelly called cytoplasm. The variation in cell size; number and shape of nuclei; variation in material content of the nuclei and cytoplasm, are all different for the different types of cells examined. Also, none of the first cells have survived the ravages of 3 billion plus years of time. Our look at a cell will be very general and based on the advanced cells of our own time.

The nucleus is usually round to slightly elongated and has its own delicate membrane enclosing its granular suspensions and fine ribbons of chromosomes. It seems to control the acquisition and assimilation of materials for continued metabolism of the whole cell. The chromosomes are tiny strings of DNA molecules that represent the genetic code building-manual for the plant or animal represented by the cell.

Cytoplasm varies more in parts and structures than the nucleus because it is where the special functions of material conversion - breathing, feeding, waste separation, cellulose and calcium assembly and extrusion etc. - are carried out. Animal cytoplasm contains a granual or rod, sometimes paired, called the centriole, which is activated during cell division and seems to act as an off-center focus for the assembly of chromosomes just prior to the cell splitting in two; the centriole may also be associated with a flagellum (whip-like tail) or cilia (hair-like filaments) that help a cell move in its environment. The cytoplasm may also contain very fine thread-like structures, called myofibrils in muscle cells and neurofibrils in nerve cells. Other small bodies are chloroplasts found in the outer cell layers of green leaves and within a few bacteria; mitochondria are small specialized bodies that sometime associate in linear groups and produce various enzymes used in the oxidation of food by the cell; they appear to be the energy source that powers the different activities or functions of a cell. There is evidence that in some cells (including human), mitochondria, centrioles and chloroplasts have their own, simplified and different, DNA genetic code! Vacuoles are globular cavities filled with clear liquid - in one-celled animals they contain food and water during digestion and help control the salt content of the cell - in plant cells the single vacuole may be very large for the storage of water; lysosome, golgi body, endoplasmic reticulum, ribosomes, pigment granuals, material storage granuals and secretory granuals are other special forms of cytoplasmic contents. Most of these particles have their own enveloping membranes which mediate the interchange of materials. They may be thought of as "organells" - organs of a cell that serve the same specialized functions as the organs (liver, kidney, lungs, etc.) of a large multi-celled animal.

Most cells are enclosed in a plasma membrane which is usually regarded as a specialized function of the cytoplasm itself. It is extremely important in regulating the cell contents because it acts as a physical barrier which is selectively permeable, allowing some substances (molecules, ions, salts, etc.) to pass freely into or out of the cell while blocking the passage of others. Outside this peripheral membrane, a cell will often construct an outer wall of cellulose in plants or protein in animals. The outer wall can also incorporate carbohydrate chitin, silica, calcium carbonate (limestone of coral reefs and porous limestone of chalk), keratin, (horn, nails, claws, hoofs of mammals).

Many of the constituents of cells are in the colloidal state i.e., very small particles in a liquid suspension. Because of their small size and great number, these small particles provide a large surface area for the adsorption of materials. Animal protein and plant cellulose depend on the adsorption of water for their activities.

Diffusion through animal or plant membranes is negligible for substances (e.g. proteins) in the colloidal state while for true solutions (e.g. sugars and dissolved gases) diffusion is virtually uninhibited. Small electrical potentials exist across the membranes that separate the various colloidal suspensions of the organelle (small specialized structures within the cell), or the peripheral membrane that encloses the cell and separates it from its environment. The electric potentials provide the energy gradient that mediates the transfer of nutrients into and through the cell, and transfers waste products and control substances (hormones, enzymes, etc.) out of the cell. All living things, the 5th state of matter, are made up of colloidal material and are sustained by colloidal processes. Smooth, mucous covered tissues of protein hold back the large albumin protein of our blood plasma while allowing oxygen and carbon dioxide to exchange/ transfer through the gas-permeable membranes in the lungs. Everything we eat (almost) is in the colloidal state. Colloidal chemistry is involved in all our food processing, clothing whether natural or synthetic, and most of our structural materials like wood, bricks and concrete, pottery and porcelain.

The activity of microbes to elephants or algae to men is all dependent on colloidal matter and process. Surprisingly few people have even heard the word "colloidal", fewer still know what a colloid is. Its importance to life is that its electrical gradients help drive the material interactions that result in the moving, inter-active, self-sustaining and self-reproducing bits of matter we have come to call living cells.

Next to the charge on the particles, the principle characteristic that makes the colloidal state so hyper-active is a physical property; surface area. A colloid is basically any small particle, usually microscopic in size that is held in continuous suspension in any support fluid. If the tiny particles actually dissolve (salt or sugar etc) in the medium (water), the particles, which disappear, are then called a solute, the medium a solvent and we end up with a solution. When the tiny particles (proteins, fats, etc.) don't dissolve and don't settle out, we have a colloid.

In a living cell, the tiny particles may be different kinds of proteins and lipids (fats) and the support medium may by a solution of salts or sugars in water. In some cell compartments the internal fluids may be quite clear because the suspended solids can be smaller than a wave-length of light - we would need an electron microscope to see them.

You may recall that surface area decreases as the square of the reduction in the radius. Well that is only true in terms of mathematical relationships of a single spherical dimension. If we consider the total surface area of a sphere as it is divided into many separate pieces, just the opposite happens - total surface area increases dramatically, compared to the original sphere. When a particle is divided in half, each half has a surface area smaller than the original particle, but the sum of the surface areas of both halves is greater than the surface area of the original particle! As each half is again halved, the surface area of the whole increases by an even greater amount. Because a colloid has many thousands of tiny particles suspended in it, the surface area presented by those particles is millions of times greater than if those same particles were in one lump. Surface area is very important to the life process because that is where the inter-change of material takes place. The respiratory volume of our lungs is only 8 liters or 1.75 gallons but the surface area, due to folding, is about 56 square meters or 600 square feet! A cubic centimeter of activated charcoal, because of its large porous surface area, can actually adsorb (not absorb as a sponge does, but adsorb) a greater volume of chlorine gas at room temperature and pressure, than can be contained in a cubic centimeter of chlorine in its liquid state. Think about it! A physical impossibility in our mesoscopic world is a normal occurrence in the microscopic world.

Material interactions in the atomic, molecular, ultra-microscopic and microscopic worlds that support the mesoscopic world of sensory man are just now beginning to be slightly understood. We are slowly coming to understand that our bodies are not separate from, but part of and immersed in, the universe as a whole. Life in all its varied forms is the 5th state of matter and man is in it, part of it, not separate from it.

Simple plants, (lichen and moss), were already securely rooted on land before animal life shook the water from its skin, about 400 million years ago. Insects and ferns evolved about 350 million years ago and the first wings appeared about 50 million years later on insects. Reptiles began evolving from amphibians about 340 million years ago. Mammals first evolved about 225 million years ago but didn't amount to much until about 65 millions years ago, when the dinosaurs suddenly died out, flowering plants appeared, birds began to proliferate, and the large land mass of Laurasia began to break-up into the continents we know today as North America and Europe.

The transition of animal life from sea to land involved enormous problems associated with structure. Skeleton; with movable parts that could support and still allow movement inside a water tight skin to prevent evaporation of internal fluids. Breathing; absorption of air through the skin is only viable for internal organs less than one quarter inch from the skin surface, beyond that requires a circulatory system. Volume of an animal increases by the cube while its surface area increases by the square. Animals larger than about half an inch in cross-section need a circulatory system and some kind of lung to absorb oxygen from the air. Temperature control; water temperature changes little between night and day, while air temperature will fluctuate considerably. Communications and interactive control; without water to carry chemical messages that identify and locate food, prey, enemies and mates, existence of the individual and the species was much more difficult on land. The meat-eaters exemplify the problem of interactive control: for any given species to proliferate, it has to avoid eating its own members and yet still be coaxed to approach its opposite sex for species reproduction.

It is the communication and interactive feature we are interested in because it eventually leads to language in man. Cell interaction and control has been chemical ever since the life process began and it remains so today. All the activity of our human internal environment, skin, lungs, brain, etc., are controlled by various chemicals. But the transition from water to air severely limited chemical messages between separate animals. Food and mate seeking are much impaired without chemical markers.

Taste and odor sensors are closely related in that they are both tactile molecule detectors. That is, both require contact with a few molecules of a particular substance before they are activated. They were used for cell and animal interaction hundreds of millions of years before electromagnetic (light) or mechanical pressure (sound) waves surpassed them (in some animals), in the ability to carry information. Taste and smell are still used today to pass specific control messages within a species.

In most animals below man, odors given off by females, in time of estrus (heat), trigger specific sexual behavior in adult males of the species. These odors are complex chemicals called pheromones, and help to illustrate that the chemical messages passing between animals of the same species are of the same order and kind as the chemicals passing between and controlling the action of, the various organs inside an individual animal. That is, chemical molecules (e.g. hormones, neurotransmitters, vitamins, etc.) are the information carriers between cells, between groups of different cells, and between cells and organs, of a single individual. They can carry specific stop or go messages, for control purposes, within a single, multi-organ body.

As evolution produced separate complex individuals, it was still necessary to get the separate male and female animal together for sexual reproduction. Chemical messages could still be used to trigger a specific response between two separate animals of the same species. In some animals, the rat for instance, this pheromone activates a "species" reproductive behavior that will only yield to "individual" survival behavior (eating) just prior to death. A male rat, given the choice between food or a female rat in estrus will choose the female and forego eating. This will continue until the male can barely stand. The female pheromone activates a reproduction compulsion (2nd program) in the male that will only be over-ridden by self-preservation (1st program) at the last possible moment.

Because human-kind seems to be one of the few animals where no sex pheromone appears to be operating, much time and energy has been spent in trying to find if there is at least a vestige of one. We've already named it an aphrodisiac in anticipation. The perfume industry would be most happy to be able to produce a sex pheromone that would work on either the female or male. Human females, when living in a close group, become synchronized in their monthly fertility periods. Although no causative agent has yet been found, it is reasonable to suspect that they are reacting to a shared chemical pheromone that is placing their individual fertility rhythms in phase.

In addition to the great utility of smelling out prey or enemies and in food selection, many animals use odors to mark out their living-room (territory) with urine or musk, from special scent glands. Termite colonies are known to be controlled by chemical messages issued by the Queen into the nest-air as odors or passed as tastes between members of the colony. Most of these messages are very specific and can change activity of food or type of food gathering, to nest building; or from closing openings to reduce hive heat-loss, to making new openings for improved air circulation.

Moths and butterflies are so sensitive to a particular pheromone that they can be triggered by a single molecule of its substance! The point to be made is that chemical messages are very good carriers of information because they are very specific. This is particularly true for an animal's internal environment where control is subconscious. The messages cannot be misunderstood because they are not received in the intellect or mind, to be analyzed or debated. They are received by specific sensors configured to detect and respond to only one type of molecule. Each sensor will trigger its own particular response mode that may initiate any one of many activities; from a brief search for a flower or an all consuming tenacious search for a mate, depending on the complexity of the multi-organed animal involved.

For a human child below age one, a whiff of smoke has no significance. It learns, over many years of instruction, that the various response modes required will depend on the circumstances currently in effect. The average adult human will have quite a different reaction to the smell of smoke at 3AM on the 27th floor of a high-rise, than the smell of smoke at 3PM while strolling down the street on a quiet fall day. In man, as in no other animal, the sound pattern he understands as the word "smoke" will evoke the same reaction as the "smell" (chemical info) of smoke itself; *provided* he has complete trust in the integrity of the source of the sound. In a crowded movie theater, the single sound "fire" can trigger the rapid exodus of hundreds of individuals - a single molecule (chemical message) could trigger no more than one individual, because it stays with its receptor.

The ability of the land animals to detect frequency vibrations carried by the air became a potential substitute for the distribution of chemical messages in water. Sound waves; a new vector of evolutionary control between individual animals became available, and was exploited. The pressure detector already evolved in the liquid medium became more important as a vibration detector in the gaseous medium.

Sound became an important operator in natural selection between land dwelling animals. It could be used to locate prey or mates in the dark or when vision was obscured. It could be used by the prey (or reluctant mates), by not making noise, to avoid detection. The absence or presence of sound became a factor in individual and species survival. The press of circumstance began to favor the more sensitive "ear" when all other factors where in balance.

A significant weakness in sound, as compared to chemical com-munication, is that of stimulation. All that a sound can do is barely vibrate a membrane which is then detected and transmitted chemically to a brain, which then must decided what, if anything, to do with the information. Chemical messages will act directly on specific receptors that can then initiate a chemical cascade, inside the animal, controlling specific long-term responses; such as, smell of food or sex pheromone will initiate particular behavioral sequences. A chemical message between individuals need not be processed intellectually by the brain in either individual; where as a sound message between individuals must be processed intellectually by the brain of at least one of the participants. The ear, like all other sense organs, connects directly to the brain. It is the brain that selects from a learned-response menu-of-available-activity, the appropriate action to initiate. The ability to initiate sounds (i.e. vocal cords) only became significant after the ear/brain mechanism was in place and seems to have reached its highest refinement in birds and mammals.

Fish and reptiles are basically silent but amphibians (frogs and toads) and insects can be quite noisy when properly stimulated. Most, if not all, mammals can produce sounds but rarely do so unless under stress. Man and birds are obvious exceptions; both are very vocal. That birds are communicating seems certain but the content is unknown. That other mammals are communicating with sound (wolves, seals, prairie-dogs, whales, dolphins, monkeys, elephants, etc.) also seems certain, but again, content is unknown.

Of all animals, Mans' use of sound for communication is by far the most sophisticated, but this sophisticated communication is only possible with those in the same language-group. However, he finds difficulty in communicating to "foreign" members of his own species only makes sense when it is understood that language is a sound-code that must be learned. The fact that he cannot communicate with foreigners of his own species, (i.e. he hasn't "learned" their language) helps to clarify why he cannot communicate with other species; we have to learn their sound-code in order to communicate. The slightly odd belief that communication with an extra-terrestrial is possible, while even a short chat with his cousin the chimpanzee is so far impossible, suggests that man does not really understand yet what language is. Genetically speaking, man has a 99% match in arrangement of DNA code with the chimp, and we are similar in structure (body) and habitat (earth). Until we can communicate with a brother animal on our own planet, man doesn't have a hope in hell of communicating with something really alien.

There is little mystery left in our understanding of how movement and motion takes place in large, multi-cell animals like mice and men. The gross movement of limbs that propel us over the ground is accomplished by rhythmic contraction and relaxation of muscles securely fastened to bone on either side of a rolling-hinge joint. That the muscle-tone is a happy compromise between automatic and conscious control, via nerve pathways, is fairly well understood. The major impasse regarding the understanding of cell movement is the peculiar propensity of the human brain to keep offering various excuses for not accepting something that is patently obvious - that cells and animals move by natural laws and not by deities or spirits! That the mouse will move out of the hot desert sun into a shady spot, the same as a man (mad dogs and English men were exempt from this natural law while residing in 19th century India) is not contested. What are debated are the principles that move "animals" and men. Mans love of self is some how diminished with the acceptance that he is animal and not "spiritual". For man it is a continuing battle of the rational mind balanced against the emotional body; the sensory information that the earth is flat and motionless balanced against the intellectual knowledge that it is neither; the childhood memories of the mysteries of life balanced against the adult awareness of death, with no intermediate stage of understanding either. In the 14th century, an expression of the idea that a dog, a pig and a man where all identical in material composition would have been answered by a visit with the inquisition. In the 20th century we understand that cellular concept to be true, but modified by our new knowledge of what a fertilized egg-cell is doing.

Each fertilized animal cell is a miniature factory that takes nutrients from its environment and assembles them into multi-cell animal structures. If we were to look down onto one of man's industrial complexes, we could see several separate factories that were each producing a different product. Each building might appear identical in general material and shape, with only minor variations in things like door size or number of smoke-stacks. Each factory would be taking in the same types of materials of iron, steel, copper, rubber, water, air, etc., but the output of each factory is different; one produces automobiles, one cranks out airplanes, and another might produce diesel engines. Inside these factories we might find that many of the work operations are being performed by automatic machines that are being controlled by computers, which are converting a coded information signal into the fabrication and assembly of various parts. These factories are made by man; as is the coded information that controls the factories output. These factories and their functions are not the product of chance - a great deal of planning and expertise went into their construction and operation. These factories and their products are the result of knowledge of the controlled manner of material interaction that man has managed to accumulate over the centuries; man is learning to control cause and effect in material interaction.

Each fertilized animal or plant cell is a tiny factory made by nature, for nature, from nature. Each is programmed with the same genetic material arranged in varying order, which represents an acquisition and assembly code of materials commonly located in the cells environment; the program has evolved through natural selection, as mediated by time, mechanical and chemical laws and availability of materials.

There are many people who cannot bear to think of themselves as animals. They cannot believe that the life they hold so dear is only sustained by the eating of other living things - salt and water are about the only things we ingest that were not once part of, or produced by, another living organism. Even the oxygen we can't live without is a gift from our plant friends. Mans body cannot produce its own protein without consuming the protein assembled by other living things. Other living things must die for you to live. For self-centered man, animals are horrible, filthy, hairy, "things" that have no table manners at all, defecate on expensive rugs or lawns and are stupid and ugly besides. Many people are insulted if they think you think they are animals. And of the precious few who do understand that they are animals and cellular in structure, and do appreciate the unwitting contribution of lower animals to our dinner-plates, there are fewer still who wish to give up the concept of "free-will", and consider that their "activities" have even a hint of instinctive or conditioned-response behavior. The concept of life as the 5th state of matter can help ease the emotional burden of intellectual truth; man really is an animal and a natural part of the planet earth and the universe. This is our home; we have evolved into it over several billion years. Your entire body is the result of a single fertilized animal cell.

What speaks more for order and precision than the genetic code as expressed by the DNA molecules in the chromosomes of all cells! It took one billion years for a "simple cell" to evolve from the primordial ocean, and it will take another 3 billion years for several of these cells to evolve into the multi-organed body of man; in terms of time it appears that the single cell is no less complex than the multi-cell animal. I say several of these primitive cells because the modern cell seems to be a symbiotic relationship between the centrioles, chloroplasts & mitocondrion organelle, that have their own DNA, and is separate from the DNA that embodies the bulk of the larger nuclei of the cell. The mitocondrion supplies the enzymes that control the reactions of biological oxidation - metabolism in the cell as a whole; it is the power supply.

Although bacteria and human sperm where first observed in 1683, they where thought of as "wee beasties", not cells. It wasn't until about 1839 that man began to understand that these and many other strange things where in fact single cells; and that all the living things around him, plants and animals, where all multi-cell organizations. It wasn't for another 120 years before he began to grasp the incredible complexity and diversity expressible by various single cells; that his entire multi-billion cell body is actually engineered by the chemical genetic code of a single microscopic fertilized cell!

Every cell (except the sex cells) in the human body carries the complete genetic code for that body. As the individual grows from the multiple divisions of the fertilized cell, groups of cells form that specialize as various organs or support and connective structures that make up the body as a whole. Your eyes, brain, ears, heart, blood, skin, everything, are all the result of a chemical code controlling the assembly of material from the cells external environment into billions of replicas that then take on the specialized co-operative functions of the organs of a complete animal. Even the eye and skin color is encoded; all in a single cell! The genetic code read-out, as expressed by every living thing, is a brilliant display of ultimate order in the cause and effect interactions of matter, at the atomic and molecular level. It leaves the mind stunned and its sensory web trembling to consider that some of that genetic chemical code has been translated, without error, for 3 billion years of time and through countless zillions of sequential cell divisions.

As you can see, with even this simplistic overview of cells, the single cell is already a co-operative composite of other smaller organelles carrying out separate activities that lead to a single body capable of maintaining the integrity of the whole; and then reproducing a copy of itself, including its manipulative contents. "Life" is clearly a sub-cellular process that is reproducing itself at the cell level; life begins below the level of the cell. We call it DNA.

The assignment of the cell as the "unit" of life, or the 5th state of matter, is quite arbitrary because life is an assembly process of matter and not a "thing". The cell, not life, is a unit thing of which there are tens of millions of different types of units. It is the cell which expresses those qualities of the 5th state of matter we call life. Some of those qualities or characteristics are: Motility (self movement), Reproduction (duplicating itself by selective assembly of material from its environment), adaptability (inherited and acquired accommodation to its total environment), Irritability (sensing and reacting), Secretion (producing one or more type of substance, such as hormones, vitamins, enzymes, etc.), Conductivity (chemical, nerve messages), Contractility (muscle movement).

These main characteristics are used to express or achieve the two basic activities of a cell or multi-celled organism; feeding and reproduction. Feeding is required for self-preservation and reproduction is required for species-preservation. If you can understand that life is not a thing but a continuity of process, you can appreciate that self preservation and species preservation are two sides to the same coin of animal or plant evolution.

The ancient ones didn't know anything about the elemental structures of the material world that went into making up molecules and compounds. They knew nothing of the cells that came to be formed from the carbon, nitrogen, oxygen and hydrogen complexes of amino acids; that in turn make up the polypeptide strands that incorporate other materials such as, sulphur, iron, calcium, iodine or phosphorus to make up the proteins, carbohydrates and fats, that make up the typical cell. They could never have dreamed that the human body was made from billions of exact copies of the same cell; that then formed groups of cells that specialized as various organs to make up the body as a whole synchronized, multi-function unit. They saw "living" matter as different from "dead" matter. They saw animals, and eventually plants, as being separate from, but living in, a natural (dead) world.

The ancients perceived themselves as so different and special, that they must have been created in the image of a deity. It was the only rational explanation of their being in this strange place they called Earth. They were not animals or part of the natural world; they were separate from but "lived" in the natural world. The ancient ones had no idea why animals had parts like hearts, lungs, livers or brains. Because his own heart and lungs moved, he supposed the mysterious "self" or spirit was located in the chest, where the soul was.

The idea that language had anything to do with awareness wouldn't occur for thousands of years! When the Egyptians interred their mummified dead, the heart, lungs and intestines were carefully stored in sealed jars for use in the after-life; the brain was not preserved, its true function was unknown. The ancient Greeks thought the brain was some kind of radiator to cool the blood; they also imagined that thought, spirit and the "spark of life" were located in the chest. That the heart was the source of life appeared rather self-evident because it could be cut out of a living animal and still continue to move while the host body was immobile and dead. It was only the slow accumulation of facts and knowledge over centuries that allows us in the 20th century to recognize that man has in fact an animal body made up of living cells. Before Humans evolved there was much that did not exist in the universe for the simple lack of a sensor to respond to it, a brain to remember it, and an audio linguistic code to word-tag it for future reference. The invention of language made knowledge, and then understanding, possible.

Chapter 6
Summary:
Who are you?

Who are you? OK, I won't keep you in suspense any longer. Now to answer the question that has dogged your mind from the very beginning of "your" existence - who are you? The answer is, in a single word, language! **"You" are language.** Easy enough to say. The sky hasn't fallen and "you" are still here

Language is mankind's greatest invention and "you" are a serendipitous artifact of that linguistic code.

But it is quite another thing to understand. If you feel the answer is silly or still don't understand it, all I can suggest is that you re-read the section on language. If you had not already guessed the answer than all I can do is apologize for wasting your time.

No need to continue further as you will not understand, let alone accept, the new universal view that unfolds from the truth that "you" are an expression of the English linguistic code. "You" are an abstraction; do not exist outside the 5th dimension. For those of you curious enough (not "willing") to go along with the concept, we have a bit more to say about the structures in the brain, and how we learn language, before we try to tie everything together.

The true double lobed brain appears only in bilaterally symmetrical animals. Its highest development is in vertebrates. The average weight in man is about 48 ounces, or 3 pounds, which is probably why brain volume and weight are usually given in metric units as 1450 cc or 1360 g respectively - both sound much bigger than 3 pounds.

The perception and coordination of the various stimuli and the voluntary control of the body takes place in the gray matter of the brain; a quarter inch thick mat of fissured gray-pink tissue that is the outer surface of the brain. This outer layer of the cerebrum is called the cerebral cortex and is composed of unsheathed nerve cells, called gray matter. Its surface area is about two and a half square feet and it weighs about 20 ounces. This cap of flesh and bare nerve-cell bodies has six layers of cells and some ten thousand miles of connecting fibers per cubic inch. An estimated ten billion cells make up its neurons of three principle types: pyramidal, spindle and stellate cells. Under this thin cap is the white matter made up of sheathed, or myelinated (it is the fatty – myelin sheath that is white) axons that interconnect various sections of the cerebrum, and the cerebral cortex itself with other parts of the brain.

A massive fissure from front to back splits the cortex into two halves which are joined by a connecting white nerve fiber mass called the Corpus Callosum. Associate Fibers run through the white matter to inter-connect the different areas of each hemisphere and a fan of Projection Fibers run from the inner surface of the cortex cap into nerve bundles entering the brain stem of the spinal nerves - they carry impulses to and from the brain.

At birth, the sensory receptors at the body surface respond to their appropriate stimuli but the nerve impulses of the detected changes do not necessarily reach the brain. Only those sensory and motor-control nerves essential for survival are responsive at birth. As the body matures, responses change and nerve conduction begins to spread throughout the individual. Nerve conduction is pretty well limited to those nerve path-ways that are myelinated; have developed their myelin sheaths and are thus specialized for very fast nerve impulse conduction. The white fibers in the cerebral hemispheres do not all receive their myelin sheaths at the same time. At about one month before birth the afferent (sensory) fibers between the cerebral cortex and the somatic or body areas of the brain stem and hippocampus begin to myelinate. Next the afferent fibers from visual and audio sensors to the cortical perceptual areas are innervated. The efferent (motor) cerebrospinal fibers of the voluntary nervous system do not begin to myelinate until about the tenth week after birth and is completed about the second year, when the child is walking. Therefore, all movements and responses made by a child up to the first two months are reflex actions and depend on the brainstem and the spinal nerves. Even though the cochlea is fully developed and the cochlear nerve is fully myelinated, reflex action is the only possible response to sound-waves. The Associate Fibers of the brain are the last to be myelinated and this is not completed till the 18th or 20th year. .

Primary linguistic centers of the left cerebral cortex.

Either right or left hemisphere of the cortex may be controlling speech, but the left cortex is usually dominant.

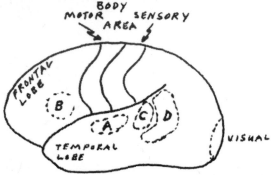

A. **Primary Auditory Center**. Where nerve impulses are perceived as "sound". Auditory nerve impulses from the Cochlea end up here. All "sounds", including those of words, begin here. Prior to perception at the Auditory Center, "sounds" are only nerve impulses initiated by air compression and rarefaction, or bone conduction of vibrations, to the cochlea where the stimuli is sensed by the Organ of Corti which converts the physical movement (vibration) to nerve impulses. Damage interferes with perception of all sound.

B. **Broca's Area**. Lies next to the brain motor area that coordinates movement of vocal cords, tongue, jaw, and lips. Controls the flow of words from brain to mouth. Can articulate up to 200 syllables per minute. Damaged; Either no speech or words very difficult and slow to utter. Sentences cannot be spoken. Damage to connections between the Broca and Wernicke areas, allows patient to hear and think clearly, but speech is meaningless word-like sounds.

C. **Wernicke's Area**. Associated with speech comprehension. All sounds reach the Auditory Center but Wernicki's Area appears to be where certain sounds are recognized as "words". Damaged; Language rhythm sounds normal but many words are nonsense phonemes and sentences have no meaning.

D. **Angular Gyrus**. Seems to bridge the gap between the words we hear and the words we read and write. Damaged; Patient can repeat words heard but not words read!

Ninety-seven % of patients with language dysfunction have suffered damage to the left hemisphere. However, very young children with left hemisphere damage may still acquire language skills because the right hemisphere takes over to compensate for the loss.

Neuroscientists believe vocabulary is stored throughout the sensory areas of the brain, each connected to the language centers because whenever there is brain damage there is usually a naming disorder. Somewhere, perhaps distributed, lies the mechanism by which the brain links its auditory centers with other sensory areas such that each object, thing or event is "named". Then all the characteristics of the thing - visual, sound, tactile, olfactory, taste, size, weight, shape, etc. are all associated in sensory memory with that "name" (abstract symbol and sound pattern).

The gray matter of unsheathed neurons and white matter of sheathed axon pathways make up the cerebrum, or new brain. It is the largest part of the brain and controls all conscious activities of the body. It is the voluntary sensory and motor control center as well as the memory, thinking and speech control area.

The cerebellum or old brain is a smaller mass of nerve tissue tucked under the back portion of the cerebrum and hugging the brain stem that inter-connects the new brain to the spinal cord. The cerebellum controls balance and regulates muscle tone. It manages the precision and fine control necessary for smooth voluntary movements such as walking, running, skating, dancing, painting or writing. It provides the coordination for our activities.

The brain stem or medulla oblongata is the reptilian brain. It receives sensory signals and transmits motor signals. All motor nerves to or from the brain pass through the medulla which controls; automatic involuntary movement, all smooth muscle, digestion, swallowing, breathing, blood vessel constriction, and reflex actions.

Nestled in front of the cerebellum and between the cerebrum and the brain stem is the Limbic System - a primitive region found in all mammals. It occupies about 20% of brain volume and seems to be the seat of passion. Emotions of fear, anger, euphoria, lust, and grief appear to be triggered or sensed in this region. Through conscious control a person can usually resist or suppress the urges and desires that come from this old mammalian brain. Part of the limbic system includes the hippocampus that has some control over the storage of long term memory, and thus is essential for learning.

Removal of the hippocampus causes the effect that old memories remain available and short term memory is functional, but no new information from the short term memory is added to the long term memory. A patient's speech and hearing are not impaired but long sentences are rambling because the focus of any conversation is soon forgotten. The same magazine may be read day after day but there is no memory storage of its contents - it is a new experience each time. Custodians and new acquaintances are forever strangers.

Emotions of pleasure or sadness are things of the moment -not remembered in long term memory. Each day is totally new and yesterday totally absent. The individual is cut-off from a remembered past-continuity by an ever widening gap of forgotten yesterdays.

The hypothalamus is another very important organ of the Limbic System. Richly supplied with blood, the hypothalamus provides the sensations or feelings of pleasure, guilt, hunger, thirst, aggression, rage and sexual arousal. Nerves extending down to the pituitary gland secrete a hormone releasing factor and thus controls body growth, sexual development, and body metabolism (the rate at which the body burns its fuel). The hypothalamus establishes the bodies "set point" of feed-back control of blood temperature and many other chemical and neuronal equilibriums. Heat sensitive nerve cells near the front of the organ monitor the human body's blood temperature for an optimum 37 deg. C.

Animals which have had a small "U" tube inserted into the hypothalamus help demonstrate its control of body response to blood temperature change. If cool water is passed through the tube, the hypothalamus will respond by increasing blood sugar level, which then increases the metabolic rate of mitochondria in every living cell in the body. This causes an increase in blood temp, but the artificial cooling tells the hypothalamus it is still too cold, so a second defense is called into action. All major skeletal muscles of the body are caused to have cyclical spasms triggered by the automatic nervous system. This involuntary shivering generates more heat from muscular contraction and is the first visual sign of hypothermia. Even though the room temp, and animal skin temperature is normal, the body is responding as if it where freezing. If the water temp, in the "U" tube is a bit warmer than the hypothalamus set point, the animal will begin to stretch-out and "pant" in order to reduce its sensed blood temperature.

When you set the room thermostat for comfort, you are relying on the skin mounted thermal sensors to determine what that temperature will be. But it is the "set point" of the thermostat in your hypothalamus that is establishing the relative interpretations of the skin sensors (the hypothalamus sets and maintains the blood temperature. The skin heat sensors determine if the environment is "warm" or "cool" relative to the body temp.), and thus the final setting you select for the room thermostat has actually been determined by your hypothalamus!

The hypothalamus also has tiny sense organs - receptors that monitor glucose and salt content of blood, and initiate feelings of hunger and thirst that stimulate a range of learned corrective actions to take that will alleviate the urge. The human learned-response-range triggered by just these two tiny urges has created an infrastructure in modern society that boggles the mind. From animal feed-lots and slaughter houses, agricultural production, processing and distribution facilities; to huge dams, aqueducts, reservoirs, wells, water control and distribution; and the professions and industries that support, maintain and extend these infrastructures. All because of two microscopic sensory cells located in the brain of an animal that is a product of the 5th state of matter!

An incredibly complex web of inter-relationships, yes; yet how can any rational mind see chaos in the infinity of ordered precision that lies right before our very eyes! Every cause has its effect and nothing, absolutely nothing, is out of place.

The hypothalamus also coordinates our body's reactions to danger by nerve impulses that control the release of hormones from the endocrine system; the fight or flight reaction. The brains perception of some threat to the body's security innervates the hypothalamus to initiate a chemical cascade that places the body in top physical readiness for what ever is to come.

Stimulated by the hypothalamus the pituitary gland releases the stress hormone ACTH that will cause the adrenal glands on the kidneys to activate. These produce even more ACTH along with other hormones that begin converting fats and proteins into sugar. Adrenalin and noradrenalin step-up heart rate and blood pressure; breathing gets deeper, bronchial tubes dilate, digestion slows down to conserve energy and more blood is shunted into the external body to improve energy supply to the muscles and cooling. The iris of the eye dilates and eye lids open wide to allow maximum viewing. In just seconds the whole body is ready to provide peak performance in either flight or fight.

Consciousness itself appears to be distributed in a tangled, densely packed, cluster of nerve cells and fibers called the Reticular Formation located in the central core of the brain stem, from the spinal cord to the middle of the brain. Nerve bundles interconnect cortical neurons with the reticular formation and with spinal cord nerves. The axons of the nerve cells of the reticular formation are very short and it can both transmit and receive signals. When messages from this formation are reduced, we sleep! Injury here can cause a coma from which the brain may not awake. The reticular formation seems to select or highlight those sensory signals and motor control signals that occupy an activity being pursued, or of interest to, an individual. It allows us to concentrate on a narrow range of specialized activity without the distraction of hundreds of other stimuli being received that are not germane to our purpose. Once the attention is focused, one becomes almost unconscious of unrelated stimuli. It may take several calls to get their attention; then there is a momentary disorientation as they look about and a short flare of crankiness - just like being disturbed from a pleasant sleep!

A typical neuron may have 150 thousand to 200 thousand dendrites within which there may be established one thousand to ten thousand synaptic interconnections with other cell's dendrites or axon terminals. Many of these connections form during the brain's early development in the fetus - they are inherited. Some of these synapses are inhibitory, tending to prevent or suppress the firing of the receiving cell. Synapses that cause or promote a neuron to fire are excitatory. The moment to moment interplay of excitatory and inhibitory synapses regulate when or if a given neuron will fire. In addition, the build-up of certain proteins in cell cytoplasm or membranes, such as the calcium sensitive enzyme PKC also affects the cell's action potential. Chemical neurotransmitters, such as acetylcholine, and their inhibiters, are also essential because signals cannot cross the synaptic gaps without them. Chemical interaction is as important as the physical dendrite cross-connections in so far as learning and memory storage is concerned.

In other words, the dendrite connections - most stimulated into formation, or at least activated, by environmental stimuli -establish the range or capacity of total patterns that can be expressed in any unit group of neurons; while the manufacture and storage of protein molecules - under control of frequency and duration of neuron stimulation - may represent the "memory" of that same group of cells. All of the stimuli patterns would fall within the web of dendrite inter-connections and the most frequently encountered stimuli pattern (memory) would be represented by the highest protein accumulation in those cells stimulated.

If you would understand yourself and where you are going, understand that the brain is where you are coming from. Understanding without knowledge is impossible. No one can "give" you understanding - you must take it. It's up to you.

There have been many analogies of how the brain does what it does. They range from ordered arrangements of books, by topics, on library shelves, through roles of microfilm or magnetic tape to index cards or punch-card files, to memory chips in digital computers. My favorite is the lighted bill-board because it can produce abstractions from physical reality - which is what the brain does. Here, a large number of tiny light-bulbs are arranged in vertical and horizontal rows. By directing electricity to any one bulb, it will light. By selecting certain multiples of lamps to light, we can create what appear to be straight lines; horizontal or vertical or any angle in between. We can create circles or squares or any shape, such as - letters, numbers, geometric shapes, animal or vegetable shapes - any pattern we like. With careful control of current flow, we can produce shading and so produce life-like images.

With proper sequencing controls, we can even make these images appear to move about or grow smaller or larger. But these images cannot move off the billboard any more than the images of our "mind" can leap from our brain. These images on the billboard are not real. The light bulbs, sockets, wire, electricity and light are real, but the images are illusions. If we light up the letter "A" we can see that it is just a particular sequence of bulbs that give the illusion of two slanted vertical lines joined in the middle by a short horizontal line. If we move very close to the sign we can see the apparently solid lines dissolve into individual dots of light arranged in a row. So, although we can create images, we can see that the images created are "apparent" and not real. Very much like a newspaper picture is made up of individual dots of ink. From a distance, our eye-brain makes it into an image and we see a face. An ordinary film picture has the same character but the dots are microscopic silver particles that have been selectively blackened by a photo-chemical process. You would need a microscope to see the silver oxide dots.

It is possible that the brain makes up its impressions, in its separate sensory compartments, by the discreet activation of a pattern of nerve cells. The pattern becomes "set" after repeated applications of the same stimuli promote dendrite interconnections between separate, but simultaneously stimulated, neurons. The dendrite growth is not by chance but stimulated by the activity of the several separate neuron cells, being activated by nerve impulses from sensory organs. The truth is we don't know how the brain does it. A famous Montreal neurosurgeon, a leader in his field said, "After fifty or so years of study, I have come to the conclusion that the brain cannot possibly do what it does!" The analogy of the brain to a lighted billboard is a very poor one. The neurons do not light up like little light-bulbs and they are not arranged in neat rows or activated by current flow. What it does demonstrate is that abstractions - things that are not real - can be created by physical matter that exists in a material universe.

The 5th dimension occurs by the chemical process of, and in, the 5th state of matter, we call "life".

Mind, as a concept, is a spin-off from the concept and fact of memory, and all thoughts are expressed by language. Phrases such as, "mind what I say", for "take note of" or "remember". And "remind me to do that" for "don't let me forget" - point to the fact that we subconsciously understand that mind and memory are one and the same. We don't know how it does it, but the brain has experiences imprinted into its cellular structure. Perhaps even its molecular structure - some experiments with mice, where a trained brain is ground up and injected into an untrained mouse, seems to indicate that the mouse that received the ground brains learns faster. A "pattern" of neurons could not survive the grinding, but molecular structure could.

Even more amazing is that we appear to have conscious, controlled, random access to these memories and then can re-associate them any way we can imagine - without loosing the original impressions! In this way we can come up with speculative conclusions, about things we have never experienced, that are sometimes correct or close to being correct. We call it reasoning or deductive/inductive rationalizing, or simply "thinking" when we refer to a problem we are working on. When trying to find the car keys we don't say we are thinking, we say we are trying to "remember where we put them. Remembering and thinking are different.

Memory is a gift. Thinking is learned. Memory is a characteristic of all vertebrates and comes with the brain. Thinking is what the human brain is doing with language - remembered sound patterns we call words, that we started learning when children. We learned to associate these words (sound patterns) with real things so well that we often confuse the word with the thing. When we learned new words for things that are abstract - not real, such as Santa Clause - we later come to realize how difficult it can be to separate reality from abstraction. Words seem so solid and real themselves, its hard to accept that the meaning of all words is assigned, arbitrary, and abstract. And as if that where not bad enough, we invented it ourselves! How can anything so contrived have any meaning at all?

Memory is the basis of all coordinated activity of life forms from single cell to man. The faculty of memory has been operational from the very first forms of nucleotides that combined to make the first nucleic acids before life began. A "chemical" memory for the configuration of amino acids into protein strands, molecule by molecule. While the strands were busily duplicating themselves they where also intermingling and finding associations both favorable and unfavorable. Those associations that proved favorable dominated and allowed the formation of ever more complex protein groups. One day, one of these groups cooperated internally and divided to make two identical, but smaller, groups - cells - and the unit of the 5th state of matter was born.

This chemical memory was not consciousness on the part of the cells' ingredients. The hydrogen, carbon, oxygen, nitrogen, sodium, chlorine, phosphorus, etc., hooked-up in every way that was physically possible for the conditions of heat, pressure, density and radiation that prevailed. When the "correct" molecular combination was reached, it simply duplicated itself so efficiently that the other combinations began to be used-up as a kind of chemical food by the more successful proteins. When the first "cell" division finally occurred about 3 billion years ago, mother and daughter cell would have found them selves in a perfect feeding environment.

The cell which ate its offspring (or vice versa) would not survive as a species. But the same could be said for the "process" that produced the cell; "natural" selection began in the valance bonds of the nucleotides of the 5th state of matter. Those cells which did recognize their family would have increased their numbers at an incredible rate and population crashes must have been frequent, until a cannibalistic bent could be refined to feed on the hoard of cells that got their energy from the non-living environment. The carnivore cells obtained their energy in enriched form, from the energy synthesizer cells.

Memory is the base from which all our other mental abilities rise. It is the base for our concepts of time, past present and future. Without memory, the symbol crunching ability of language, and therefore thought, could not take place. We cannot "learn" if we cannot remember. Remembering what a word symbol means makes communication possible. To "know" something means our mental ability to recall it - we remember it. Most humanists feel confident in saying that sight is the most important sense because it appears that about 70% of our information is channeled through our eyes. Indeed, we often resort to drawing pictures when trying to explain something. This is a misconception that helps highlight the subtlety of the audio symbols by which we speak, listen, learn and think. We use these audio symbols (words - language) so casually we are not even aware that we are doing it. Like breathing, language use is so "natural" we are not normally aware that we are doing something very unique. We learned to speak the audible symbols of a linguistic code only because our brain can remember sound patters as "words"; not the visual patterns of the written word, but the audible patterns of the spoken word, in order to "think". Without the brains ability to remember sound symbols, "thinking", and intellectual activity if you like - would be severely limited.

All multi-organed creatures have some kind of brain because that is what we call the area having the densest concentration of dendrites, ganglia and nerve cell nuclei. Only the vertebrates have a "true" brain. That is, a brain similar to mans, because, in the final analysis, all "meaning" is referenced back to man the species and man the individual - you. Through natural selection it has become the organ of mediation between other organs for the benefit of the whole creature.

I avoid the word "control" (in place of mediation) because that suggests a conscious guiding or internal selective awareness, and that is not the basic function of the basic brain. Its basic function is inter-communications between the other organs and the external environment to secure a favorable match.

Trapped between a rock and a hard place, the internal and external environment, the brain is shaped by the press of variable circumstances into a narrow response mode defined by the limitations of its body organs. In other words, the animal whose sensory awareness and adaptability is overwhelmed by external change cannot survive. Through eons of evolution the brain, like all other organs, has been crafted by the cause and effect of material interaction to fit snugly into its own niche in the multi-organ animal that carries it.

That the whole animal evolves into, and with, its ecological niche by the inter-action of the animal with its environment is fairly well understood. Even though we are now aware that animals are multi-cell, we often ignore that they are also multi-organed, and that it is the very special symbiotic relationship between these organs that make-up the animal as a whole - encased in its largest and most visible organ, the skin. The evolution of an animal is, of course, the adaptation of the whole animal. All of the organs are involved, including the brain. The animal body is a micro-environment to the organs and they evolve within that micro-environment - in much the same way as a species evolves into its external macro-environment. The animal is not simply reacting to its external environment. It is responding internally, as well as externally. The animals' external environment is no less "alive" than its internal environment. The animal affects nature as much as nature affects the animal. The animal is nature. Nature is the animal. The animal is immersed in the natural world. Its biomass feeds from and is nourished by the external environment and then gives back nourishment. The animal is not separate from but part of the natural world. Man and the world are one.

When we are first born there is no conscious memory. Memory, in terms of information, doesn't exist until information is put in. The input to the brains memory is via the sensors and the only type of information that comes streaming down the connector nerves are "blips". All sensors are sending the same code. The brain gets around this by having the various sensors feed separate brain areas and then acknowledging these different areas in a chemically, or "emotionally" different way. What the brains sensors are detecting are changes in the stimuli being received. The sensory receptors are "tuned" to the stimuli, but it is the changes in some quality of the stimuli that is being detected.

The ear is tuned to a frequency range but it is the sequential variation of amplitude, frequency, and Doppler shift between ears that are being transmitted to the brain by a train of ionic chemical waves that vary only in frequency. The brain does not respond to a single pulse - it must have a train of pulses before the brain will become cognizant that a "change" is taking place. The eye is tuned to a frequency range but it is the changes, in some quality, of the stimuli that is being detected and then pulsed to the brain.

The human brain is responding to changes in the stimuli and not the stimuli itself. Only the sensory organ is responding to the stimuli and each organ then translates the variations (changes) of those stimuli into discrete pulses for the brain. The brain gets only a stream of frequency variable pulses from any and all its sensors. That is all it has ever gotten. That is all it "knows" - tiny ionic waves pulsing up its nerve fibers. And the brain begins to "remember" as patterns begin to emerge and set, in the response sequence of inter-connected cells.

As the sand ripples of a river bottom are a response to the repeated rippling of waves or the callous forms where skin is rubbed, or the complex over lapping interference patters are recorded in a hologram, the neuronal response to repeated streams of blips, is a distributed pattern of inter-connections that allows the same neurons to be stimulated every time a "familiar" pattern of blips is received. The brain "learns" by these "remembered" neuronal patterns. In an operating room, if these discrete groups of cells are physically probed or electrically stimulated, the individual may "remember" some sensory experience.

Memory is in the "patterns" of neurons and dendrite interconnections of the brain. The brain cells and their propensity for inter-connection, as guided by repeated patterns of stimuli, are gifts of biological evolution over billions of years of time. All vertebrates, not just man, embrace this gift; make use of this gift. The patterns in which the neuronal axons, dendrites (branching side extensions of neurons) and ganglions (clusters of nerve fibers) inter-connect are directly related to non-fatal response activity.

For example, an 18 month old child may gleefully stagger onto an express way to get a better look at the things that are whizzing by - totally oblivious to the danger. If the child is properly trained and its memory is normal, it "knows" by its 4th year that road-ways are no-no's (mom or dad will give you a smack if you go too near the road) even though the child is still unaware of the danger. Where ever a response pattern does not result in some form of injury, continued growth and learning is possible. Any pattern that leads to a fatal or serious injury response is automatically self-terminating.

Another example; we have considerable voluntary control over our visual organ. Even though, as adults, we have learned to control the eye-in-socket position and the lens curvature, for depth-vision, we did not "consciously" learn how to direct and focus our eyes at the age of six-months. In fact, before we are aware of our "selves" (about age 2 or 3 yr) we are not aware that we can actually override these auto-controls and deliberately cross our eyes or defocus them, thus momentarily leaving ourselves "blind" - without a visual image. Because there are no serious after affects of this playfulness, we can get away with it.

We cannot take voluntary control of the iris opening because evolution has weeded-out those few who could. Ok, probably could, there is no way of knowing for sure. If we could put a voluntary override on our iris, we could do irreparable damage to the retina. Since the retina, the light detector and transducer, is what the eye is all about, Mother Nature has not had to weed-out those of us who played with positioning or focusing muscles, out of context with their design and function - the retina (the purpose) was not being harmed. But anyone playing with the iris risked serious damage to the retina due to intensity over load.

Even in natural conditions the retina is constantly getting sectional intensity over-loads due to reflections from water, glass and other shiny surfaces. Early and late in the day the brilliant disc of the sun is constantly popping into the visual field. The iris is normally shuttered several stops below optimum conditions for viewing because the eye, as an organ responsible to the retina, has been selected by evolution to protect its responsibility. Keeping partially closed, consistent with safe viewing, is the way to function in a world that gives sudden surges of light intensity. When you see something that catches your interest, the iris automatically opens a bit to allow maximum visual acuity.

Behavioral studies have noted this tiny, unconscious, indicator of mental interest in humans. Advertisers are actively engaged in consumer studies to try and produce the container whose shape and color is most appealing to the largest sampling of people. Special cameras photograph customer's eyes - and iris opening - as they pass various products. The iris gets measurable larger when the brain sees something of "interest".

So, just as your natural mother will give you a shout or a clout to keep you out of trouble 'till you acquire "common sense", Mother Nature has clouted most of our forefathers who exercised voluntary control of the iris. Any damage to the retina would decrease vision, and therefore performance, in food gathering or distinguishing a small grassy mound from a striped tiger's side.

At a more subtle level of influence in natural selection, sound patterns - words - have come to be associated with "things" in the natural world of human hearing perception. The word "nose" is a particular sound-pattern that the English language brain has learned - after hours and days and weeks of repetition, to get the pattern "fixed" - to associate with the fleshy facial protuberance located between the "mouth" and the "eyes". The brain learns to associate sound-patterns, words, with "things" in precisely the same way it learns to "see" the light patterns - by repeated stimulation of the visual group of brain neurons - that slowly come to be understood as the word-tag "vision". All our sensory perceptions, sound, sight, touch, smell, taste, balance, etc., are learned and remembered by pattern repetition. Words are sound-patterns in air and blips in nerves that are learned, remembered; neuronal-patterns of "meaning" that allow the brain, and man, to "think".

Linguists often become so preoccupied with the "rules of grammar" and sentence structure that they conclude that there is some inner law, or some intrinsic underlying meaning, to language that ties all tongues together. But no existing language is a crude holdover from earliest time - they are all constantly growing in words and meaning. Students of language put the cart before the horse when, they marvel how we learn "grammar. They forget that their convoluted "rules" of word use are totally subjective and snobbishly arbitrary in their attempts to judge the "correct" way to speak, as done in the drawing-room compared to the street vernacular. They fail to acknowledge that the transmission of any information or idea by language is fraught with misunderstandings and misconceptions, simply because most words have several definitions. The alphabet has no consistent relation to the sounds they represent and most of the symbols have more than one sound. Also many of our phonemes require more than one letter (th, sh, etc.). That there is no rationality or logic in grammar, spelling or syntax is obvious by the end of grade school. They are fatuously pompous in their assumption that it is the marvelous culture of any admired group that has produced its language. In fact, it is the other way around.

It is marvelous language that has produced the culture. We cannot think without the words of language. We don't think with culture! There would be no culture to admire without language. *Language IS culture!*

It really does seem so self evident as to be beyond debate, but that is the magic of language. It is so indispensable and "normal" that it is easy to forget that we ourselves invented its sounds (words) and then applied those sounds as symbols (names) for things. The "things" became the meanings of the "words" and the words came to be regarded as the things themselves. We taught these relationships to our children, just as they were taught to ourselves. But the words are just arbitrary assignments of sound patterns. There is no significant difference in the babbling sounds produced by children of any linguistic group during the first six months. After this the different groups begin to diverge as each child begins to learn its native tongue by imitating the word-sounds it hears. Russian has the most phonemes at 71; English has about 43, and Hawaiian has the least at only 13.

For comparison, the Chimpanzee has about 25 different vocal sounds - these are not phonemes because the Chimp has not yet developed an abstract linguistic code. Since the tongue root and larynx has not descended in the Chimp's throat, as it has in humans, it could not reproduce human speech. If Chimps have a language, man is not yet aware of it. By two years, a child will have developed a vocabulary of about 300 words by casual conditioned response training. In all languages vowel sounds are made by larynx sounding and air flow essentially uninterrupted; consonants, air flow gets closed-off; stops, sharp start/stop of air, and fricative, partial air block to produce a hiss. Learning to speak is the most complex conditioned response learned by man.

All languages are abstract and have whatever meaning we (the brain) assigns to the sound pattern (word). Culture, whether English, German, French, or whatever, is a manifestation and direct consequence of language. The Sapir-Whorf hypothesis of around 1940 was basically, "People can think about only those things that their language can describe or express." Without words or phrases with which to articulate a concept, that concept will not occur. For example, Eskimos have 12 different words for "snow", but only one word for "tree". People of a tropical rain forest have many different words for "tree" but no word at all for "snow". For the people of the forest, a snow-house, a snow-bank, a snow fall or flake or a glacier or a blizzard is literally unthinkable. For the Eskimo the things "root, leaf, wood, branch, forest," are literally unthinkable because his word "tree" is the only sound symbol he has for anything to do with trees. The language of each describes the environment of each and the environment in turn limits the experience, and thus the word-tags that define the conceptual thoughts of each. The words describe their environment and their place in it - their culture. The languages man speaks guides his sense of reality, determines mans perception of himself and the world.

A tribe of men lives for generations in a given region. Word sounds are invented over time and attached to those things they become aware of that make up their environment. Their invented language grows with time and names everything they "know", including themselves and everything they own, body and soul. Their language defines their environment. Their language defines their culture. Their language defines their bodies and inner-selves. They cannot think without the language they invented.

A linguist's view of the societies of man is "every national language is a product of a special culture, and all individuals who use it are influenced to think and behave in accordance with that culture's values". Now, interchange the words "language" and ""culture" and see how it should read!

A child's controlled movement, babbling, sitting up, crawling walking, etc. are all dependent on the sequential enervation (myelination) of the efferent nerve tracts involved. While the tracts are being brought on stream, they are also being stimulated by use. Each repeated use strengthens muscle and connective tissue being stressed and promotes dendritic inter-connection of nerve ends that are close and being simultaneously stimulated. Maturation and learning blend into increasing coordination and progressively expanding abilities.

For the purposes of language acquisition and speech mechanism control, by which "you" come into being at about age three, the period between three months and two years is the most significant twenty-one months of your entire life. It is not what you "learn" in that period that is so critical, but the dendrite inter-connections of brain neurons that is important. The genetic code limits the neurons and establishes some of the connections, but environmental stimuli establish new interconnections and certainly activate those that are inherited. The more cross-connections, the greater will be the variety of patterns the neurons can absorb and thereby express.

The ability to recognize and interpret sounds is learnt mainly in the first twelve months of life and promotes a readiness to listen. From twelve to eighteen months is the first articulation of words which promotes the readiness to speak. Initially we have absolutely no choice over the response our ear has to a sound wave, or any other sensory cells response to its stimuli. Its response is fixed and the resulting nerve impulses are limited to that fixed response. It is the brain that learns to "listen" by voluntary control of the efferent (motor) nerves feed-back to the sensors, and then begins to remember certain patterns of frequency, amplitude, phase, quality, etc... It is the brain that stores these patterns of enhanced cells that later become the comparators, the criterion, by which all later sounds become identified. It is these growing patterns of memory that are controlling the efferent nerve feed-back, (from Cortex to sensor) to the afferent nerve/sensor system, (sensor to Cortex.)

These patterns of memory become what the sensor is "listening" for. That is how we recognize our own language. We remember the sound patterns of words and sentences by repetition. A sound pattern (word) we have never heard before leaves use befuddled because we can't respond to it. We don't know what it means.

As adults, and because our written language is phonetic, we can look up the word in the dictionary and learn its meaning. If we want to retain the word and its meaning, we have to use the word in speech, physically (speak) and/or psychologically (thinking) many times before it is locked-in for several years. Every sound, from bell to trumpet to drum to word is learned - and named. Intensity is learned and named (loud, soft, etc.). Frequency is learned and named (high, low, alto, etc.). Included in sounds recognized are human voice-sounds of singing, laughing, and speech. When the "speech" is in our learned linguistic code of sound patterns we can recognize words and their meanings from the auditory patterns stored in our "memory". Language gives understanding and all language is learned.

Of the word-classes learned, such as nouns, adjectives, verbs etc., pronouns are usually the last to come into play because in simple sentences, a noun can always be used instead. Nouns, the names of things, are the words we first learn to use. A two-year old will usually refer to itself by name or by second party (we, us,). Only after use of first party singular (me, I,) does use of other pronouns develop.

A process of dialogue is necessary for language comprehension and speech acquisition. A sickly child confined to home and reared by deaf parents was unable to speak or understand words at the age of three years - even though he had been exposed daily to television. Without the interactive dialogue of a parent or instructor repeatedly associating a name (word sound) to an object (eye, finger, ball, etc.) the meaning in words and language is easily missed. The deaf parents were as unaware as any hearing parent that their child NEEDS auditory and vocal stimulation if it is going to learn spoken language. Speech happens so naturally that it just doesn't occur to us that we LEARN to speak by imitation and practice - it will NOT happen in isolation. The child's brain was getting no clues as to "word = thing" stimuli from parents who did not speak or respond to his "voice". The TV sound was just noise; it had no meaning because no one gave it meaning. His own speech control mechanism would be atrophied due to lack of use. The lad was as linguistically deaf and speechless as the day he was born simply for lack of stimuli. The critical "natural" period for dendrite interconnection was past. He will be intellectually impaired for life. Only intensive specialized training can now force the child to "hear" and "speak" language.

A serious hearing impairment will hinder a child's normal development of speech because the ear serves as a feed-back loop to monitor the annunciation of spoken words. A severe hearing loss later in life will usually cause a corresponding degeneration of speech. A speaker reproduces the sounds he hears!

A child born totally deaf (very rare, fortunately) must be forcibly taught a visual and tactile symbolic code, that replaces the linguistic code, in order to tie together his remaining sensory inputs. If this is not done, he will end-up an idiot and will require a caretaker to sustain his life. He will NOT develop anything close to "human" intelligence if left to his own devises. That is the power of the linguistic code! It is a very difficult task for student and teacher. Where it succeeds, the child's brain learns to "think" with visual and tactile clues where the brain normally thinks with audio patterns - words. The child born totally deaf doesn't learn to "think" with words (sound patterns). It can't. It learns to associate visual symbols (sign language and written words) with real objects. The symbol for "nose" becomes a visual pattern; not a sound-pattern. The brain born deaf learns to "think" (by force) with visual and tactile symbols, just as the hearing brain learns to "think" (without force) with audio symbols.

Most dreams are strange distortions of body emotions and visual images. They normally lack a sound-track but occasionally we do dream where speech is used. Where a child born deaf has learned sign language or writing, these communicative dreams are not sounds but in visual symbols of signing and writing.

The deaf brain cannot learn or be taught in sound symbols any more than the blind brain can learn or be taught in visual symbols. Just as the deaf brain "thinks" with its learned visual code, the hearing brain "thinks" with its learned audio code.

The brain requires a symbolic code of some kind in order to "think".

The common symbol used for all human speech is audible sound patterns. The common symbolic code used by the brain to think is the linguistic code of audible speech. The normal brain cannot learn its linguistic code without the stimulation of dialogue. The brain cannot think in a linguistic code it has not learned.

Language is mankind's most unique characteristic. It is his greatest invention because mankind simply would not exist without it. Language is mankind. It is nature's greatest innovation in evolutionary adaptation since the emergence of the chemical genetic code in the 5th state of matter - life itself. Language is a common symbol audible code referenced to the brain's perception of physical reality and the abstractions generated within the brain itself. It is the very core of all other forms of human communications, whether it be comprehension of oral language through hearing (normal) or seeing (speech reading by the deaf), or the comprehension of literate language through reading and writing. All other forms of coded information, analog or digital, are referenced back to the spoken language information content. The video image so common in every home is almost useless without its linguistic component, either sound or printed word display, to give it meaning. In the normal individual it is the basis of thought itself.

"You" ARE language.

The audible codes are phonemes that come in patterns of "word sounds". Visual patterns are parallel impressions of an over-all scene taken moment by moment. Audio patterns are serial impressions of audio stimuli that are summed as a continuity of ongoing events. We can view a picture scene in one-sixteenth of a second but it takes a full 60 seconds to "hear" the Minute Waltz. However, the serial audio phonemes are learned as patterns in time as surely as the parallel pixels of visual perception are learned as patterns in space (remember how the visual field is "locked" to the skull's eye-sockets').

Now let's try to tie everything together. The universe of matter came into existence in time and space. Both space and time may be abstract. The matter persists from moment to moment of incident time. The matter interacts in periods of lateral time. Lateral time limits material interaction to the velocity of light. There is no apparent smallest time interval for incident time. The matter exists in sub-atomic form and there are many varieties of the atomic form. These different types of matter accrue into different physical states of plasma, gas, liquid and solid, depending on their energy content. Energy may also be abstract. All this material in its various states interacts in very specific ways we have come to identify as natural laws. The four states of matter blend into each other as a function of their material energy content and the energy level surrounding them. In a very narrow energy band , some of these materials interact in their gas, liquid and solid states to produce a 5th material state that is capable of absorbing energy and material from its surroundings and of reproducing itself in discreet units called genes. These genes in turn specialized and cooperated with some of their neighboring genes and began to produce copies of their cooperative groups as multi-gened cells; with a membrane to protect their contents. As the complexity of these cell units increased, their abilities to manipulate their environmental conditions in space, time and energy (all of which may be abstract - not existing) also increased. The cells began to inter-act, instead of just re-act, to their environment and thus may be regarded as one-celled organisms. A direct consequence of this increasing inter-action was a growing awareness that allowed more than one response to a stimulus, where more than one stimulus was being perceived. In other words, where more than one stimulus was being sensed, it was now possible to inhibit one or more of the responses to those stimuli. The organism was making adaptive choices and those choices that prolonged existence to the point of reproduction became the genetic code of "choice". The organism AND the environment were determining the selection process. Over billions of years of adaptive response to stimuli, the 5th state of matter - life - evolved ever increasingly complex organism's for ever increasingly complex interactions with its environments. That the adaptive response to different stimuli is infinitely variable is seen in the incredible variety of organisms, both plant and animal and from microbes to whales, that make up the 5th state of matter today.

If you think of life as a "magic spark" you will never understand what life is. Life is not a "thing", it is a chemical process. If you can accept that what we call "life" is material process that is more accurately defined as the 5th state of matter, than you can begin to understand that life is a natural part of the universe. The 5th state of matter has its own unique set of natural laws; just as each of the other four states have their natural laws of material interaction.

The animal man has evolved as part of the 5th state of matter. He is also part of the universe and not separate from it. All of the plants and animals have an adaptive fit into their environments. All the higher animals evolved a centralized nervous system that allows them a greater range of relationships with their environment. This centralized nervous system has evolved into a specialized control organ called a brain in the highest forms of animals. This brain organ is what gives man the survival edge over all other forms of the 5th state of matter. Unfortunately, unlike most other organs of the body, the brain is not "automatic".

One has to actually use the brain in order to derive any of its benefits. Thus mans survival is not guaranteed.

It is in the cortex of the human brain that we find a convenient physical reality for our lattice-work sphere of words; the physical side of our inner 5th dimension of mind. The gray-matter of the cerebral cortex is only a thin matt of tangled neurons that almost completely covers the brain. It is where man does his thinking and remembering.

It is where the words of language are stored so this is where we can place the hypothetical lattice-word sphere. Not as little printed signs or even whispered sounds within its web, but as "patterns of inter-connections" produced by the audible linguistic code and forced into the neurons material structure by incessant re-enforcement. Inside the 5th state of matter lies the potential for a 5th dimension. Only in man has the 5th dimension of mind begun to put in an appearance.

Inside the 5th dimension are the meanings of all the words that make up the structure of the lattice-word sphere. It contains all of mans loves and all of mans fears. It is the place of intelligence and reason, ignorance and chaos. It is to man everything, but its depths could not be plumbed without a mental code that sticks a "name" on everything that the brain's sensors detect. This mental code by which man thinks uses the auditory sense and the speech mechanism to generate the sound patterns (words) used to codify everything in mans known universe. The mental code calls itself language and "you".

From our vantage point in the 5th dimension, we can see that all plants and animals are parts of the same environment. They are each as much a part of the world as a rock, a mountain, an ocean or a star. Man too is part of the universe. You are not an outside observer looking in. Your body and "you" are part of it. Your fertilized cell was a continuation of the Homo sapiens DNA genetic code that has threaded its way through the bodies of your parents, their parents, and their parents, parents; that thread twists and loops invisibly through all the members of your species. It is a chemical code of order being preserved, expanded, modified and projected in living things. It is the process of material interaction of the 5th state of matter we call "life". It does not exist in the other four material states. It is brought about by an unimaginably large number of cause and effect sequences of events, which take place in materials as mediated by natural laws.

Each affect results from its cause. Not a single speck of matter or bundle of energy is anywhere but where it must be, as a result of its preceding cause. There is no random motion, no random cause, no random effect, and no random event; there is no chaos. All is order and perfection. Nothing is out of place. Whatever is, whether it be a new star in the firmament or new child on a planet called earth, it came about by a cause and effect sequence of absolute order that hasn't missed a beat in 15 billion years. Chaos is the absence of perceived order; just as darkness is the absence of light. Chaos and darkness are not "things"; they are the absence of things. Chaos "exists" only as an abstract concept in the 5th dimension; it is trapped by a material wall of natural laws and cannot affect the four dimensional space/time continuum of the real universe.

The circumstances that lead to your body's birth were not lucky or unlucky, by chance or by deity, by art or by design, serendipitous or lackadaisical. They have been orchestrated over time by a harmony of laws that have shaped a material multi-cell body for a perfect fit into its environment; a fit so perfect that the body is part of the environment's atoms and molecules; it is part of the environment. The genetic code works its wonders within the pull of a gravity field. The temperature range and atmospheric pressure of earth "cook" and "mold" our cells within their limits of variation. Your body and how it works is the chemical process of the 5th state of matter honed to perfection through 3 billion years of adaptation and an infinity of ordered sequence from the beginning of the universe.

What we think of as "our" lives is from conception through birth, then slow growth to an adult stage which persists until some critical part fails, and we die. Our lives are "little more" than the continuity of chemical process, in the 5th state of matter, that is perpetuated by an adaptable chemical code! It is only that "little more" that really has significance for man because everything else is rigidly controlled by natural laws that are in-violate - they cannot be broken.

The "little more" is what man uses to manipulate (not change or over-ride) the natural laws to produce effects that favor man's preferences. We cannot break any physical laws but we can control material interaction such that a 747 will lift off the ground, taking us with it. We can "fly" even though that ability is not assigned in our DNA code. The "little more" is what we in English call language.

Your body was not conceived or born by accident. It could only have been produced from a very specific egg and sperm cell, and any other combination of cells from your parents would have produced some other DNA code. Your body & your life can't be an accident! Even if "you" are not happy with it, it still cannot be an accident any more than the circumstances that lead to its conception could be an accident. An effect cannot exist without the cause that gave it birth. Hold-off on your judgments of good or bad, right or wrong until the end of the book. Try to understand first, then judge and evaluate to your hearts content.

From the moment of conception you are also in the grip of another code; a linguistic mental code that is controlling the conscious actions of your parents. All other things being equal, you will also learn that code and come under its influence directly. It will become more important to you than the genetic code that brought your body into physical existence. Why? - Because the linguistic code is what "you" are. The sense-of-self, what you think of as the "I" or "me" within your body, is only possible through language. What you understand as "thinking" cannot take place without language.

In 1644 Rene Descartes announced, "I think, therefore I am".

Since "I" cannot be if I cannot think - and I can not think without language - it follows that "I" must be language! "You" think of yourself as being more important than your body because the body can do nothing without "you" inside to guide it. "You" are at the controls - "You" must exist!

Sorry, but "you" are as much an illusion as "I" am. The body already has its 1st and 2nd programs of individual and species survival for the preservation of the genetic code. How do you think our pre-linguistic relatives survived? How do you think the rest of the animal and plant world survive?

"You" add greatly to the genetic codes expression, but "you" are definitely NOT essential. Language IS essential to "you" however, because "you" cannot be without it. In fact the only reason "you" and "I" can even be communicating is because we have both been trained, by conditioned response, to recognize the same abstract linguistic code of "meaning". I am as much a victim of this code as you are.

"We" are both abstract, we are not real! We persist as patterned codes in the lateral time of memory in the 5th dimension of the dendrites and neurons of the cerebral cortex.

The following is pure speculation. I offer it only in the interest of promoting understanding. The original utility of an audible code was to replace the chemical code-carrier of water, between separate land animals. Millions of years of adaptive response selection, between the internal and external environment of each animal, proved audible signals to be extremely useful to both the hunter and the hunted. The utility of deliberate sound production, to capitalize on the auditory sense within a species - as opposed to echo location - came only after the hearing sense was locked into the genetic code. In birds and mammals the ability to vocalize became a tool of reproduction and thus "sounding" behavior also became translated into the species DNA survival code. In at least some of the birds and mammals, a partial reflex-arc or neuronal inter-connection between the hearing and sounding abilities occurred. This allowed the animal to mimic the sounds that it heard and thus "play" with its sounding abilities. Because feed-back is the very root of control, and thus mediates everything that is happening in a successful life form, the brain needed no special prompting from the DNA code to make use of this new feed-back loop. That is, the body could now produce and control stimuli (sound) that one of its sensors could detect. It slowly learned to associate natural sound-patterns (i.e. not words) with other stimuli (sight, taste etc) that it was becoming aware of. This was NOT language; just a growing awareness that sound was associated with other sights, tastes, smells and touch of things.

About 250 thousand years ago a primate attached a particular voice sound to a particular object and that sound-pattern became the word-symbol for the thing. By 100 thousand years ago our brain had reached its present size and we probably had about 200 "words" plus body-awareness (recognize our reflection).

By 40 thousand years ago we humans were beginning body adornment, cave art, and probably had physical body awareness, and a vocabulary of 300 words. Language had begun and what we think of as modern man appeared on the earths' landscape.

Between 30 and 20 thousand years ago man became aware of his own mortality (began burying his dead) and began his forays into abstract thought with a vocabulary of about 800 words. End of speculation.

Because words are meaningless sounds until at least two people can agree on what they represent, the invention of language could not take place overnight. Language grows as new perceptions force man to devise new words or refine the old. It is a very slow process.

In our modern world, body awareness comes into existence at about 2 years of age, as indicated by recognition in a mirror and an active vocabulary of about 300 words. At about 3.5 years, and approximately 1200 spoken words, inner self awareness (and "you"), come into being, as indicated by shyness. By 4 years of age you are speaking in short sentences with about 1550 spoken words and starting to ask a lot of "what's that" questions.

The early "you" is not really thought of as a separate thing. It is more like a "body-you". When told you have a "soul", you think of it as a separate thing inside your body. Something besides "you", in there.

"You" start to separate from body-self to inner-self in the teenage years of turmoil. As you enter puberty you are getting strange urges and the body is doing things you haven't asked it to do and that it never did before. They are embarrassing because of our puritanical society. You have lots of questions you would like to ask but no socially approved words to express them. You start to question the meaning of words and the existence of self and soul and creator; you begin to skate near the edge of the mental black hole.

The idea that words and life have no meaning frightens you as insane and meaningless itself; so you never go near the mental black hole again. By the time your 18 or 20 the sense of "you", as separate from your body, is complete. But you don't suspect that language has had any part to play in the musings of your mind. One trip to the edge of the mental black hole was enough. You may by now suspect that "I" and "soul" are in fact one, that the "inner self" is really your soul. But that will depend on your religious instruction and gullibility rather than expertise with language. There are many more words yet to learn and many adjustments to word meanings yet to come before one becomes comfortable with language.

If you are now able to say "I cannot think without language", then step with me to the edge of the mental black hole. Step up to the lip of its mighty maw and look into the 5th dimension of mind.

Can you see all the abstractions swirling about in its ebony void? All the meanings of words "you" have learned are in there because all words are assigned, abstract, symbols! Mathematics and music and language and good and bad and indifferent, and right and wrong and maybe and up and down and in-between and left and right and middle, and beauty and justice and millions of other abstractions are floating around in there.

Physical things like rocks and trees and animals and galaxies do not exist in there - only the meanings of their word-symbols are abstract.

There is no reality within the 5th dimension created inside the lattice-work sphere of words - all is illusion. There is Santa Clause (we even capitalize "his" name!) and the tooth fairy and the Cheshire cat and look, there's "you". You are right at the source of the vortex. "You" are the source. Come, step a little closer to the brink and you can see stars and whole galaxies of stars glimmering in the velvet darkness.

Watch with the minds un-shaded eye the intense pulse of a supernova as it spews out more energy in twenty seconds than the rest of the visible universe combined. See the new dawn of a new universal view. We are standing at the brink of a new understanding of the universe and your place in it. What does it mean you ask? It means the universe is alive and beginning to contemplate itself.

This is the end of my little work, not the end of the story of language. You are more than just a figment of your imagination. You are the source; the namer of all things; the beginning of a new understanding; an effect changing into a cause.

Your presence is felt in the 5th dimension inside the 5th state of matter that persists as a collection of microscopic flecks on a speck of dust orbiting a single star in a small galaxy of stars within a universe of billions of galaxies. You are not an accident and you are part of it. "You" may be the first stirrings of a universe becoming aware of itself; the dawn of a new beginning.

Best Wishes for good health, happiness & good fortune,

James H. Washer

Glossary

Aether: is a concept, historically, used in science (as a medium) and in philosophy (as a substance). Any number of aether theories in alchemy, natural philosophy, and modern physics which suppose a "fifth element". Luminiferous aether, in early physics considered to be the medium through which light propagates

Angular gyrus: is a region of the brain in the parietal lobe, that lies near the superior edge of the temporal lobe, and immediately posterior to the supramarginal gyrus; it is involved in a number of processes related to language and cognition. It is Brodmann area 39 of the human brain.

Broca's area: is a section of the human brain that is involved in language processing, speech or sign production, and comprehension. Broca's area is named after the 19th-century physician Paul Broca. The concept of Broca's Area was originally produced with the intent to explain how speech production was inhibited in the learning of communication by the deaf; however, it is currently used to describe many anatomical aspects of psychological processing mechanisms.

Catalaze: To modify, especially to increase, the rate of (a chemical reaction) by catalysis.

CCD: A charge-coupled device is an analog shift register, enabling analog signals (electric charges) to be transported through successive stages (capacitors) controlled by a clock signal. Charge coupled devices can be used as a form of memory or for delaying analog, sampled signals. Today, they are most widely used for serializing parallel analog signals, namely in arrays of photoelectric light sensors. Not all image sensors use CCD technology; for example, CMOS chips are also commercially available.

Centriole: is a barrel shaped organelle found in most animal eukaryotic cells, though absent in higher plants and fungi.The walls of each centriole are usually composed of nine triplets of microtubules (protein of the cytoskeleton).

Chloroplasts: are organelles found in plant cells and eukaryotic algae that conduct photosynthesis. Chloroplasts absorb light and use it in conjunction with water and carbon dioxide to produce sugars, the raw material for energy and biomass production in all green plants and the animals that depend on them, directly or indirectly, for food. Chloroplasts capture light energy to conserve free energy in the form of ATP and reduce NADP to NADPH through a complex set of processes called photosynthesis. It is derived from the Greek words chloros which means green and plast which means form or entity. Chloroplasts are members of a class of organelles known as plastids.

Ciliary Muscle: is a muscle in the eye that controls the eye's accommodation for viewing objects at varying distances.

Cochlea: is the auditory portion of the inner ear. Its core component is the Organ of Corti, the sensory organ of hearing, which is distributed along the partition separating fluid chambers in the coiled tapered tube of the cochlea.

Cochlear duct: (or scala media) is an endolymph filled cavity inside the cochlea, located in between the scala tympani and the scala vestibuli, separated by the basilar membrane and Reissner's membrane (the vestibular membrane) respectively.

Corpus Callosum: is a structure of the mammalian brain in the longitudinal fissure that connects the left and right cerebral hemispheres. It is the largest white matter structure in the brain, consisting of 200-250 million contralateral axonal projections. It is a wide, flat bundle of axons beneath the cortex. Much of the inter-hemispheric communication in the brain is conducted across the corpus callosum.

Cytoplasm: The protoplasm outside the nucleus of a cell.

Dendrites: Many branches off a nerve cell near a neurons nucleus. Usually conducts signals into the cell.

Endoplasmic reticulum: or ER, is an organelle found in all eukaryotic cells that is an interconnected network of tubules, vesicles and cisternae. These structures are responsible for several specialized functions: protein translation, folding and transport of proteins to be used in the cell membrane (e.g. transmembrane receptors and other integral membrane proteins), or to be secreted (exocytosed) from the cell (e.g. digestive enzymes); sequestration of calcium; and production and storage of glycogen, steroids, and other macromolecules. The endoplasmic reticulum is part of the endomembrane system. The basic structure and composition of the ER membrane is similar to the plasma membrane.

Endolymph: is the fluid contained in the membranous labyrinth of the inner ear.

Enzymes: are biomolecules that catalyze (i.e. increase the rates of) chemical reactions. Almost all enzymes are proteins. In enzymatic reactions, the molecules at the beginning of the process are called substrates, and the enzyme converts them into different molecules, the products. Almost all processes in a biological cell need enzymes in order to occur at significant rates. Since enzymes are extremely selective for their substrates and speed up only a few reactions from among many possibilities, the set of enzymes made in a cell determines which metabolic pathways occur in that cell.

Fifth Dimension – See mind

Fifth State of Matter – All living things – life. The unit of which is a cell or assembly of co-operative cells that exchange materials and energy with its environment for its growth, maintenance and mobility and reproduces itself. It persists in two mainly symbiotic groups named plants and animals, and is a natural part of an evolving universe.

Golgi apparatus: (also called the Golgi body, Golgi complex, or dictyosome) is an organelle found in most eukaryotic cells. The primary function of the Golgi apparatus is to process and package the macromolecules such as proteins and lipids that are synthesized by the cell. It is particularly important in the processing of proteins for secretion. The Golgi apparatus forms a part of the endomembrane system of eukaryotic cells.

Ivan Petrovich Pavlov: (Russian: September 14, 1849 – February 27, 1936) was a Russian physiologist, psychologist, and physician. He was awarded the Nobel Prize in Physiology or Medicine in 1904 for research pertaining to the digestive system. Pavlov is widely known for first describing the phenomenon of classical conditioning.

Language: An audio-phonetic code that humans have invented in order to assign a name, or word-tag to everything known, real, experienced or imagined.

Laurasia: was a supercontinent that most recently existed as a part of the split of the Pangaean supercontinent in the late Mesozoic era. It included most of the landmasses which make up today's continents of the northern hemisphere, chiefly Laurentia (the name given to the North American craton), Baltica, Siberia, Kazakhstania, and the North China and East China cratons. The name combines the names of Laurentia and Eurasia.

Life: See the Fifth state of matter.

Lysosomes: are organelles that contain digestive enzymes (acid hydrolases). They digest excess or worn-out organelles, food particles, and engulfed viruses or bacteria. The membrane surrounding a lysosome allows the digestive enzymes to work at the 4.5 pH they require. Lysosomes fuse with vacuoles and dispense their enzymes into the vacuoles, digesting their contents. They are created by the addition of hydrolytic enzymes to early endosomes from the Golgi apparatus.

Malleus: or hammer is a hammer-shaped small bone or ossicle of the middle ear which connects with the incus and is attached to the inner surface of the eardrum.

Mesoscopic: For the practical purposes of this book, (the occurrence of an inner self), the mesoscopic world, the world "we", "I", live in, is defined by the detectable changes that occur within the stimuli that activate our natural, unaided sensors. (No artificial enhancements like Microscopes, telescopes etc.)

Mind: A sensory affect caused by the activation of patterns in groups of neurons of the cerebral cortex in some animal forms, mainly humans, resulting from a learned condition-response imposed by a tribal generated audible linguistic code. This sensory pattern creates a fifth dimension with the already acknowledged 4 dimensions of the space-time continuum. It is the location of the individual "sense of self" within the 5th state of matter.

Mitochondria: In cell biology, a mitochondrion (plural mitochondria) is a membrane-enclosed organelle found in most eukaryotic cells. These organelles range from 1–10 micrometers in size. Mitochondria are sometimes described as "cellular power plants" because they generate most of the cell's supply of adenosine triphosphate (ATP), used as a source of chemical energy. In addition to supplying cellular energy, mitochondria are involved in a range of other processes, such as signaling, cellular differentiation, cell death, as well as the control of the cell cycle and cell growth. Mitochondria have been implicated in several human diseases, including mental disorders, cardiac dysfunction, and may play a role in the aging process. Their ancestry is not fully understood, but, according to the endosymbiotic theory, mitochondria are descended from ancient bacteria, which were engulfed by the ancestors of eukaryotic cells more than a billion years ago.

Several characteristics make mitochondria unique. The number of mitochondria in a cell varies widely by organism and tissue type. Many cells have only a single mitochondrion, whereas others can contain several thousand mitochondria. The organelle is composed of compartments that carry out specialized functions. These compartments or regions include the outer membrane, the inter-membrane space, the inner membrane, and the cristae and matrix. Mitochondrial proteins vary depending on the tissues and species. In human, 615 distinct types of proteins were identified from cardiac mitochondria; whereas in murine, 940 proteins encoded by distinct genes were reported. Mitochondrial proteome is thought to be dynamically regulated. Although most of a cell's DNA is contained in the cell nucleus, the mitochondrion has its own independent genome. Further, its DNA shows substantial similarity to bacterial genomes.

Mitochondrial DNA: (mtDNA) is the DNA located in organelles called mitochondria. Most other DNA present in eukaryotic organisms is found in the cell nucleus. Nuclear and mitochondrial DNA are thought to be of separate evolutionary origin, with the mtDNA being derived from the circular genomes of the bacteria that were engulfed by the early ancestors of today's eukaryotic cells. Each mitochondrion is estimated to contain 2-10 mtDNA copies. In the cells of extant organisms, the vast majority of the proteins present in the mitochondria (numbering approximately 1500 different types in mammals) are coded for by nuclear DNA, but the genes for some of them, if not most, are thought to have originally been of bacterial origin, having since been transferred to the eukaryotic nucleus during evolution. In most multicellular organisms, mtDNA is inherited from the mother (maternally inherited). Mechanisms for this include simple dilution (an egg contains 100,000 to 1,000,000 mtDNA molecules, whereas a sperm contains only 100 to 1000), degradation of sperm mtDNA in the fertilized egg, and, at least in a few organisms, failure of sperm mtDNA to enter the egg. Whatever the mechanism, this single parent (uniparental) pattern of mtDNA inheritance is found in most animals, most plants and in fungi as well. mtDNA is particularly susceptible to reactive oxygen species generated by the respiratory chain due to its close proximity. Though mtDNA is packaged by proteins and harbors significant DNA repair capacity, these protective functions are less robust than those operating on nuclear DNA and therefore thought to contribute to enhanced susceptibility of mtDNA to oxidative damage. Mutations in mtDNA cause maternally inherited diseases and are thought to be a major contributor to aging and age-associated pathology.

In humans (and probably in metazoans in general), 100-10,000 separate copies of mtDNA are usually present per cell (egg and sperm cells are exceptions). In mammals, each circular mtDNA molecule consists of 15,000-17,000 base pairs, which encode the same 37 genes: 13 for proteins (polypeptides), 22 for transfer RNA (tRNA) and one each for the small and large subunits of ribosomal RNA (rRNA). This pattern is also seen among most metazoans, although in some cases one or more of the 37 genes is absent and the mtDNA size range is greater. Even greater variation in mtDNA gene content and size exists among fungi and plants, although there appears to be a core subset of genes that are present in all eukaryotes (except for the few that have no mitochondria at all). Some plant species have enormous mtDNAs (as many as 2,500,000 base pairs per mtDNA molecule) but, surprisingly, even those huge mtDNAs contain the same number and kinds of genes as related plants with much smaller mtDNAs.

Myelin layer: The main consequence of a myelin layer (or sheath) is an increase in the speed at which impulses propagate along the myelinated fiber. Along unmyelinated fibers, impulses move continuously as waves, but, in myelinated fibers, they hop or "propagate by saltation." Myelin increases resistance across the cell membrane by a factor of 5,000 and decreases capacitance by a factor of 50. Myelination also helps prevent the electrical current from leaving the axon. When a peripheral fiber is severed, the myelin sheath provides a track along which regrowth can occur. Unmyelinated fibers and myelinated axons of the mammalian central nervous system do not regenerate.

Neurofibrilla: a fine proteinaceous fibril that is found in cytoplasm (as of a neuron or a paramecium) and is capable of conducting excitation.

Organ of Corti: (or spiral organ) is the organ in the inner ear of mammals that contains auditory sensory cells, or "hair cells."

Organelle: In cell biology, an organelle is a specialized subunit within a cell that has a specific function, and is separately enclosed within its own lipid membrane. The name organelle comes from the idea that these structures are to cells what an organ is to the body (hence the name organelle, the suffix -elle being a diminutive). Organelles are identified by microscopy, and can also be purified by cell fractionation. There are many types of organelles, particularly in the eukaryotic cells of higher organisms.

Ossicles: (also called auditory ossicles) are the three smallest bones in the human body. They are contained within the middle ear space and serve to transmit sounds from the air to the fluid-filled labyrinth (cochlea). The absence of the auditory ossicles would constitute a moderate-to-severe hearing loss.

Perilymph: is an extracellular fluid located within the cochlea (part of the ear) in 2 of its 3 compartments; the scala tympani and scala vestibuli. The ionic composition of perilymph is comparable to that of plasma and cerebrospinal fluid. The major cation of perilymph is sodium.

Ribosomes: (from ribonucleic acid and "Greek: soma (meaning body)") are complexes of RNA and protein that are found in all cells. Ribosomes from bacteria and archaea are smaller than the ribosomes from eukaryotes, although all three domains of life have significantly different ribosomes. Interestingly, the ribosomes in the mitochondrion of eukaryotic cells resemble those in bacteria, reflecting the evolutionary origin of this organelle. The ribosome functions in the expression of the genetic code from nucleic acid into protein, in a process called translation. Ribosomes do this by catalyzing the assembly of individual amino acids into polypeptide chains; this involves binding a messenger RNA and then using this as a template to join together the correct sequence of amino acids. This reaction uses adapters called transfer RNA molecules, which read the sequence of the messenger RNA and are attached to the amino acids.

Saccule: is a bed of sensory cells situated in the inner ear. The saccule translates head movements into neural impulses which the brain can interpret. The saccule is sensitive to linear translations of the head, specifically movements up and down (think about moving on an elevator). When the head moves vertically, the sensory cells of the saccule are disturbed and the neurons connected to them begin transmitting impulses to the brain. These impulses travel along the vestibular portion of the eighth cranial nerve to the vestibular nuclei in the brainstem.

Self – The concept or belief of an "inner being" produced as a side effect or artifact of language.

Synapse: the point at which a nervous impulse passes from one neuron to another

Syrinx: (Greek for pan pipes) is the name for the vocal organ of birds. Located at the base of a bird's trachea, it produces sounds without the vocal cords of mammals.[1] The sound is produced by vibrations of some or all of the Membrana tympaniformis (the walls of the syrinx) and the Pessulus caused by air flowing through the syrinx. This sets up a self-oscillating system which modulates the airflow creating the sound. The muscles modulate the sound shape by changing the tension of the membranes and the bronchial openings.[2] The syrinx enables some species of birds (such as parrots, parakeets, and mynas) to mimic human speech. Unlike the larynx of mammals, the syrinx is located where the trachea forks into the lungs, and because of this some songbirds can produce more than one sound at a time.

Tectorial Membrane: Covering the sulcus spiralis internus and the spiral organ of Corti is the tectorial membrane, which is attached to the limbus laminae spiralis close to the inner edge of the vestibular membrane. The tectorial membrane partially covers the hair cells in Organ of Corti and vibrate when fluid sound waves hit it.

Vacuoles: are found in the cytoplasm of most plant cells and some animal cells. Vacuoles are membrane-bound compartments within some eukaryotic cells that can serve a variety of secretory, excretory, and storage functions. Vacuoles and their contents are considered to be distinct from the cytoplasm, and are classified as ergastic according to some authors. Vacuoles are especially conspicuous in most plant cells.

Utricle: or utriculus, along with the saccule is one of the two otolith organs located in the vertebrate inner ear.

Vestibular system: is important in maintaining balance, or equilibrium. The vestibular system includes the saccule, utricle, and the three semicircular canals. The vestibule is the name of the fluid-filled, membranous duct than contains these organs of balance. The vestibule is encased in the temporal bone of the skull.

Wernicke's area: is a part of the human cerebrum that forms part of the cortex, on the posterior section of the superior temporal gyrus, encircling the auditory cortex, on the Sylvian fissure (part of the brain where the temporal lobe and parietal lobe meet). It can also be described as the posterior part of Brodmann area 22, and, for most people, it is located in the left hemisphere, as the left hemisphere is specialized for language skills. Occlusion of the middle cerebral artery in a stroke can affect the proper functioning of this area. Wernicke's area is named after Carl Wernicke, a German neurologist and psychiatrist who, in 1874, discovered that damage to this area could cause a type of aphasia that is now called Wernicke's aphasia or receptive aphasia.

This condition results in a major impairment of language comprehension, and in speech that has a natural-sounding rhythm and a relatively normal syntax but is largely meaningless (a condition sometimes called fluent or jargon aphasia). Wernicke's work initiated the study of this brain area and its role in language. It is particularly known to be involved in the understanding and comprehension of spoken language. It is connected to Broca's area via the arcuate fasciculus, a neural pathway. It also has connections to the primary auditory cortex, evidence for its role in the comprehension of the spoken words.